ABOUT CANADA
DISABILITY RIGHTS

ABOUT CANADA
DISABILITY RIGHTS

Deborah Stienstra

About Canada Series

Fernwood Publishing • Halifax & Winnipeg

Editing: Brenda Conroy
Cover design: John van der Woude
Printed and bound in Canada by Hignell Book Printing

Published in Canada by Fernwood Publishing
32 Oceanvista Lane, Black Point, Nova Scotia, B0J 1B0
and 748 Broadway Avenue, Winnipeg, MB R3G 0X3
www.fernwoodpublishing.ca

Fernwood Publishing Company Limited gratefully acknowledges the financial support of the Government of Canada through the Canada Book Fund and the Canada Council for the Arts, the Nova Scotia Department of Communities, Culture and Heritage, the Manitoba Department of Culture, Heritage and Tourism under the Manitoba Publishers Marketing Assistance Program and the Province of Manitoba, through the Book Publishing Tax Credit, for our publishing program.

Library and Archives Canada Cataloguing in Publication

Stienstra, Deborah, [date]
About Canada : disability rights / Deborah Stienstra.

(About Canada series)
Includes bibliographical references and index.
ISBN 978-1-55266-462-9 (pbk.).–ISBN 978-1-55266-463-6 (bound)

1. People with disabilities–Civil rights–Canada. 2. People
with disabilities–Legal status, laws, etc.–Canada. 3. Human
rights–Canada. I. Title. II. Series: About Canada series

HV1559.C3S845 2012   362.40971   C2011-908399-X

CONTENTS

To those,
including Patrick Kellerman, Henry Enns,
Catherine Frazee, Jim Derksen, Ellen Chochinov
and many others, who have taught and continue to teach me
how to live well, including with disabilities

INTRODUCTION: WHAT ARE DISABILITY RIGHTS?

I am a person with a disability and living on social assistance. I find that after I pay my bills, like rent and phone and cable, I am left with $250 a month for food, household things like clothing, coffee, and anything else I might need or want to do. That works out to about $7 a day for everything. The cost of food goes up and my pension cheques stay the same. Other costs go up, like cable or phone, and my disability pension stays the same. I shop for clothes at thrift shops so I don't buy anything new. I have my clothes on today from thrift shops. I like going to Tim's sometimes for lunch or for coffee, but I often don't have any money left to do that. It costs a lot to buy healthy food. I need help to pick the right food and I need more money to buy things that will keep me healthy. I would like to have more to live on….

I would like the public to be aware that living on social assistance puts the person, that is me and many of my friends and most of our People First members, in poverty. And then when we try to work, they cut back on the assistance. And how we can buy clothes for work and pay for the transportation to get there? It is like they try to keep people with intellectual disabilities poor and dependent. We need jobs that will help us to be helpful in our communities and that will help us to live with some respect. We care that people with intellectual disabilities are still placed in institutions. Imagine how poor they are. No jobs, no going to Tim's with friends, no choices in what to eat. No way to get to be a member of groups like People First. No way to live like the rest of us here, that is, in poverty.

I'm learning that we have rights like all Canadians. While I'm not sure is if having rights will help us come out of poverty.[1] Calvin Wood, President of People First Nova Scotia

Earlier the same year that Calvin Wood wondered if having disability rights would get people with disabilities out of poverty, just before the start of the Paralympics in Vancouver on March 11, 2010, the Canadian government announced that it had ratified the United Nations Convention on the Rights of Persons with Disabilities (UNCRPD), the international agreement on disability rights. The Convention includes basic principles: respect for inherent dignity; individual autonomy including the freedom to make one's own choices; non-discrimination; full and effective participation and inclusion in society; respect for difference and acceptance of persons with disabilities as part of human diversity; equality of opportunity; accessibility; equality between men and women; and respect for the evolving capacities of children with disabilities.

These international rights echo the disability rights embedded in Section 15 of the Canadian Charter of Rights and Freedom, which came into force on April 17, 1985: "Every individual is equal before and under the law and has the right to the equal protection and equal benefit of the law without discrimination and, in particular, without discrimination based on … mental or physical disability."

Why does Calvin Wood wonder whether having these rights will help him get out of poverty? One of the major reasons that Calvin lives in poverty is because many in Canadian society think that having an impairment or condition means that he and others are not able to work at a "regular" job, that they shouldn't have children and that they are "different," often in ways that are limiting, pitiful or devaluing. The disability is actually created by attitudes and assumptions about difference and impairment rather than the impairment itself.

This approach to disability, which is often called "socially constructed" or "the social model of disability," recognizes that humanity is made up of a wide range of bodies. Through the meaning we give to these different bodies we create societies, schools, workplaces and programs that can include or exclude people. The challenge of disability rights is to recognize the ways in which we discriminate, or exclude people with impairments and conditions, and work to change so that there can be full participation, inclusion and access for all people in Canada.

The "social model of disability" was created as a response to the dominant perspective on disability, often called "the medical model of disability." The medical model says people are disabled because they have an impairment or disease. The goal of the medical model is to identify what makes individuals different from what is considered normal, whether that is a variation in their body or difference in how their bodies or minds function. Once the "abnormality" has been identified and labelled, the work is to treat, fix or rehabilitate the individual to maximize their functioning. Interventions most often involve medical or health professionals. Historically, this model has also been linked to eugenics, which distinguished "the fit" from the "unfit."

Who Are People with Disabilities?

Disabled people are us — people who work, play, go to school, live in families, raise children, are gay and straight, eat, cook, care about the environment, surf the Internet…. No matter where you look, or whom you talk to in Canadian society, you'll find a person with disabilities, or someone with disabilities in their lives.

In its 2006 survey, Statistics Canada found that 14.3 percent of the Canadian population identifies as a person with disabilities.[2] This means that more than 4.4 million people in Canada live with disabilities. More women than men experience disability, and the rate of disability increases with age. Experiences with disability are also complicated by intersections with racial/ethnic backgrounds, immigration status and Aboriginality, as well as type of impairment and activity limitation. Families face barriers and exclusion as a result of disability experienced by children, elders and other family members.

Disability is often confused with impairment or health conditions, and the language we use to talk about disability is not clear or agreed upon by all. Some people think disability is the same as impairment or chronic illness or conditions. Some think people with disabilities are ill or that disability is all about poor health. How we think and speak about disability is critical to how we understand disability and the place of people with disabilities in Canadian society.

Disability is used in this book to refer to the experiences of meeting barriers or facing exclusion as a result of living with certain bodies or bodily differences. Living in a world built for people who have sight means that blind people face barriers when they are given print documents or walk in public places with signs that are not in Braille or without curb cuts. But accommodations, including documents in Braille or available electronically, audio GPS units, Braille signs and guide dogs, all assist people who are blind to live independent lives and contribute to their communities. Others meet barriers to mobility, learning or comprehension, as well as stigma about mental

health or intellectual disability. Many people with disabilities experience barriers in more than one area of life.

Responses to Disability

Through these experiences with disability, we recognize what it is.
Disability is something that sets some people apart from others, makes
them different because of how they look, how they act, how they
move or why they need support or assistance. While we see these
variations in bodies and minds, we often assume these differences
signal "abnormality."

Those assumptions lead many of us to avert our gaze from
someone using a wheelchair or shush our children who ask loudly
why that man sounds, looks or acts so weird. They encourage us to
acts of charity for "those poor disabled children" on telethons or for
those who "suffer" with diabetes, cerebral palsy, muscular dystrophy
or some other terrible condition. We believe those people with a
disability are challenged, poor, without the possibility of work and
suffering, and we want to help because they did nothing to deserve
this "problem." Or, at least, we want to keep them from making us
feel bad about all that we do have, and we know that we do not want
to become one of them.

These negative assumptions about disability colour all of our
society, from the media portrayals of people with disabilities to the
policies created to assist them. They depict people with disabilities as
dependent, needy, expensive to accommodate, high users of health
care, sick, a burden and incapable. In short, they describe people
who are less than full and equal citizens of Canada. The Canadian
Human Rights Commission recognized this situation:

> Canadians with disabilities face obstacles wherever they go.
> Whether it is a door threshold that is too high for a person
> using a wheelchair, the absence of publications in Braille or
> large print, or inadequate tax and social security measures,

people with disabilities are far too often denied full citizenship in Canadian society.[3]

Disability rights, or the belief that people with disabilities are fully human with the rights and dignity enjoyed by all people, address the gap between the circumstances, barriers and opportunities people with disabilities, and those without disabilities, experience. The UNCRPD, adopted by the United Nations in 2006, is the most recent international agreement on disability rights. Its purpose is

to promote, protect and ensure the full and equal enjoyment of all human rights and fundamental freedoms by all persons with disabilities, and to promote respect for their inherent dignity.

Persons with disabilities include those who have long-term physical, mental, intellectual or sensory impairments which in interaction with various barriers may hinder their full and effective participation in society on an equal basis with others.

Complementing this groundbreaking United Nations convention, Canadian society has been shaped by legal decisions interpreting the meaning of disability rights in the Charter of Rights and Freedoms and as a result of complaints to human rights commissions across the country as well as to other bodies which regulate aspects of disability rights, including the Canadian Radio-Telecommunications Commission (CRTC) and the Canadian Transportation Agency (CTA).

Over the last three decades there have been improvements in the lives of Canadians with disabilities, in part resulting from these articulations of disability rights. But as Calvin Wood noted, being a Canadian with disabilities, for many, still means living in poverty, being without work, having to cover many costs that result from barriers, being out of the mainstream of communities, being invisible or forced to live in circumstances not of their own choosing and living with abuse, violence and death. Disability rights continue to be elusive for most people with disabilities, and many face discrimination in their daily lives.

In 2005, the Canadian Human Rights Commission noted that disability was the ground of discrimination in 50 percent of its cases[4] and it continues to hover at around 40 percent of cases. Marie White of the Council of Canadians with Disabilities argued in an open letter to members of Parliament in 2009 about the importance of human rights commissions: "Canadians with disabilities need Commissions to proactively remove barriers that prohibit our full and equal participation in Canadian society."[5]

Even the editorial board of the *Globe and Mail* in 2008 recognized the significance of bringing people with disabilities into the mainstream of Canadian society.

> The real question is whether Canadians are content to pay lip service to bringing the disabled into the mainstream while leaving them in effect shut inside their homes. It is a question that involves the mentally ill as well as the physically disabled. Bringing either group into mainstream life — on to regular city or inter-city buses, into subways and movie theatres and the workplace, means making actual accommodations. And paying for them.[6]

Exclusion and discrimination shape and are reinforced by both individual attitudes, cultural images and practices and structures and institutions in Canadian society. Government policies and practices, including in the areas of social assistance, health care, education, childcare, taxation, building codes, Aboriginal rights, immigration, development assistance, information technologies and housing, influence how we experience disability.

Disability rights enable people with disabilities to make decisions about their lives and future, claim rights on their own behalf, and participate actively in all areas of Canadian society. Disability rights can increase access and inclusion in critical areas like education, employment, transportation, telecommunications and health care. Disability rights also identify new approaches and practices, such as universal design, disability supports and income supports, that transform Canadian society to be more inclusive and accommodating for all Canadians.

Including people with disabilities fully in Canadian society, with the rights enjoyed by non-disabled Canadians, requires social transformation, not simply "fixing" some bodies. It requires all Canadians to recognize and redress attitudes, cultural images and policies that make people with disabilities invisible, set them aside in institutions, undermine or reject their contributions and value, and justify their neglect, abuse and death. It also calls upon Canadians to appreciate the possibilities of living a rich and complex life with disabilities, the liberating benefits of the right supports, the ways in which we all belong and the importance of relationships and caring for all in society. It involves the simple recognition and honouring of the dignity, autonomy and rights of all people, including those who experience disabilities.

1. PEOPLE AND POLICIES IN SEARCH OF DISABILITY RIGHTS

Disability rights in Canada emerged in response to a long history of exclusion, institutionalization of and paternalism towards people with disabilities in Canadian society, as Marcia Rioux, a disability studies scholar, suggests.[1] Much of that history has yet to be written but is beginning to be told by those who live with forced sterilization and other eugenic practices and by those who were institutionalized. The legacy and stories of survivors of eugenic legislation in Alberta and British Columbia are part of the Living Archives on Eugenics in Western Canada. People First of Canada and the Canadian Association for Community Living have created a joint task force on deinstitutionalization. They understand institutions as "any place in which people do not have, or are not allowed to exercise, control over their lives and their day to day decisions." Advocacy for disability rights and full citizenship began in Canada in the late 1970s and since then has had some impact on the changing policy context. Despite the advocacy of people with disabilities, their increased presence in communities, workplaces and schools and more clearly articulated policy statements of rights, people with disabilities continue to experience significant exclusion, disadvantage and marginalization in all areas of Canadian society.

Advocacy for and by People with Disabilities

Self-advocacy organizations of people with disabilities, created in the late 1970s, became the front line for disability rights in the 1980s and beyond. These organizations began in opposition to the groups of medical and rehabilitation experts that had been speaking for people with disabilities for years. In Canada, the Council of Canadians with Disabilities (CCD), known as the Council of Provincial Organizations of the Handicapped (COPOH) until 1994, is the major national advocacy organization of people with disabilities. The CCD emerged when people with disabilities were unable to get the March of Dimes and Easter Seals organizations to accept that at least half of their board members should be people with disabilities. In response, organizations of people with disabilities formed first in the Prairies and in Kitchener-Waterloo, Ontario, and then at the national level, to advocate for and by people with disabilities.[2] Canadian groups made a similar challenge at Rehabilitation International, the international meeting of rehabilitation experts, in Winnipeg in 1980. That event is widely recognized as the inception of the international movement of disabled people and a turning point for global disability rights.[3]

The initial goal of self-advocacy disability organizations was to ensure that no decisions were made about people with disabilities unless they were involved in the decision-making — exemplified in the popular slogan "Nothing about us without us." This meant pressing for representation by people with disabilities in policy-making and advocacy forums. The CCD successfully lobbied the federal government to appoint one of its leaders, Jim Derksen, as a staff member to the Special Parliamentary Committee on the Disabled and the Handicapped. Derksen used his presence there to mobilize advocacy for the inclusion of disability rights in the Charter of Rights and Freedoms.

Self-advocacy disability organizations also pressed for recognition that existing models of service provision, or care provided by health care and rehabilitation "experts," excluded and devalued people with disabilities. Delegates to the 1980 Rehabilitation International meetings in Winnipeg "condemned as human rights violations the segregation and lack of self-determination of people with disabilities perpetrated by the institutionalized rehabilitation system."[4] In response, and drawing from the United States, people with disabilities created a model of service provision managed and directed by the recipient, called "independent living." Rather than what is often called "care," service provision recognizes and values the expertise the people with disabilities have in the area of disability services as a result of their life experiences.[5] The independent living movement created local centres where people with disabilities give peer support and share knowledge on how to manage their lives and use their supports in the best ways possible. In 2010, there were at least twenty-eight independent living centres across Canada.

While independent living is the focus for many people with disabilities, people with intellectual disabilities and their families prefer to talk about "community living" and "deinstitutionalization." Advocacy by parents, especially mothers, of children with disabilities began more than fifty years ago in Canada and resulted in what is now the Canadian Association for Community Living (CACL).[6] Much of their advocacy has been directed at closing institutions, providing appropriate supports for people to live in their communities and ensuring inclusive education and supported decision-making.

Given the history of relationships between people with disabilities, service providers and condition-specific organizations, it is not surprising that advocacy related to disability involves a complex web of organizations. Michael Prince, a leading author on disability policy, notes that the disability community includes condition-specific organizations like the Multiple Sclerosis Society; service-providing organizations like the Canadian National Institute for the Blind and the Canadian Paraplegic Association; and user-led (or consumer-led, in disability community language) organizations at the national, provincial and local levels, including the CCD, People First of Canada,

Independent Living Canada, the National Network for Mental Health and many others.[7]

The diverse interests of these organizations and communities have often meant that advocacy was diffuse and directed towards many different goals. But since 2003, more than a hundred organizations, led by the CCD and CACL, have come together with a common platform and priorities, including the National Action Plan. The plan sets disability supports and deinstitutionalization as the foundation for an inclusive and accessible Canadian society. Disability supports are the supports required for daily living and may include technical aids and devices, special equipment, homemaker, attendant, interpreter and other personal services, and environmental adaptations.

> An appropriately targeted investment in disability-related supports would assist Canadians with disabilities to participate in early learning and childcare, become educated and employed, live more independently, and look after their families.
>
> Such an investment is the priority of the disability community and is the foundation upon which a comprehensive National Action Plan on Disability must be built. Central to this initiative is a commitment to deinstitutionalization and removing the stigma attached to disability.[8]

An important second step outlined in the National Action Plan is to introduce measures to alleviate poverty among people with disabilities: "The poverty of Canadians with disabilities is a national disgrace. Canadians with disabilities and their families are twice as likely to live in poverty as other Canadians and the incidence of poverty among Aboriginal people with disabilities is even higher. Existing systems of income support are failing Canadians with disabilities." This focus has encouraged anti-poverty, childcare, social justice and labour organizations to join with the CCD, CACL and other disability groups.

This united focus has galvanized disability groups to work with both the provincial and federal governments, in terms of their respective duties. The provinces are primarily responsible for disability-related supports, and the federal government can play a significant role in income support. Addressing disability in Canada is complex and requires action that recognizes not only the federal nature of government but also the importance of Aboriginal governance.

Policy Context

The net of government responsibilities for programs and services related to disability is intertwined and complex. Not only do the federal and provincial governments have separate and overlapping responsibilities, the federal/provincial/territorial ministers and officials have become an additional layer of government involvement. In general, provincial governments have responsibility for social services and education (kindergarten to grade twelve), while they share responsibility for health, employment and income security. Those responsibilities have evolved over the last thirty years, since the United Nations International Year of Disabled Persons in 1981. This section discusses the evolution of the policy contexts, and Chapter 3 looks at the effect of policies in key areas on the lives of people with disabilities.

Response to the International Year of Disabled Persons

In response to the International Year of Disabled Persons, Parliament created a committee to examine the situation of people with disabilities. With its *Obstacles* report, the Parliamentary Committee on the Disabled and the Handicapped provided stories of real people with disabilities and recommendations for removing disability-related obstacles in their lives. The committee's follow-up report focused on the unique situation of Aboriginal people with disabilities.

Several provincial governments responded to the International Year and the United Nations Decade on Disabled Persons

(1982–1991) by creating their own mechanisms to respond to the situation of disabled people, including provincial advisory councils in New Brunswick, British Columbia, Alberta, Nova Scotia and Saskatchewan.[9] In 2010 Newfoundland and Labrador came on board with an advisory council. The councils have changed and adapted over time, many becoming more embedded in government and less independent. In 2011, Manitoba, Saskatchewan, Newfoundland and Labrador, Quebec and the federal government have offices for disability issues as central bodies coordinating government policies. These also existed in Alberta and British Columbia but have been disbanded or made more diffuse within government.

Some of the most focused attention to disability issues has come as a result of tripartite initiatives. At the end of the United Nations Decade for Disabled Persons, the federal/provincial/territorial ministers of social services held a review, called "Mainstream '92," of existing disability employment, service and income arrangements. It included a lengthy and detailed consultation with organizations of people with disabilities. This review provided disability organizations an opportunity to reflect upon how well disability rights had been implemented since the Charter came into effect. The situation was not positive as Laurie Beachell, the long-time national coordinator of CCD, argued in 1992:

> Many within the disability community in the early 80's put considerable energy into ensuring that the rights of people with disabilities were protected within the Charter of Rights and Freedoms. It was felt that such protection from discrimination on the basis of disability, guaranteed within the supreme law of Canada, would remove many barriers to full participation of persons with disabilities. While realized to some extent, this hope has not resulted in major changes to the income support and service delivery systems that persons with disabilities depend upon. Certainly there have been improvements since that time. But being a Canadian with

a disability still means living in poverty, being unemployed and being served outside the mainstream by an outdated delivery system. It was hoped that Charter protection would require governments to amend legislation and programmes to ensure equality of opportunity and full citizenship, but this has not happened. Thus, in looking toward the development of a new system, the disability community once again is reiterating its message that full citizenship and equality of opportunity must be the fundamental underpinnings of the system.[10]

Given the large role for provincial governments in the provision of social services, in 1996 the federal government appointed a task force to examine its own role in disability. Led by Andy Scott, MP from New Brunswick, the task force included representatives from organizations of people with disabilities and crossed the country to ask what the federal role should be. Its report, *Equal Citizenship for Canadians with Disabilities: The Will to Act*, made recommendations related to labour market participation, income support and taxes. Some of these recommendations became part of federal/provincial/territorial initiatives on employability assistance.[11]

In the late 1990s and early 2000s, the policy work related to disability was primarily found at the federal/provincial/territorial table of ministers responsible for social services. Most significantly these ministers adopted, in the social union framework, the 1998 document *In Unison: A Canadian Approach to Disability Issues*. Quebec did not participate in the process because it wanted to retain its autonomy to make its own decisions, but it had a consistent policy framework. *In Unison* identified its vision as the following:

> Persons with disabilities participate as full citizens in all aspects of Canadian society. The full participation of persons with disabilities requires the commitment of all segments of society. The realization of the vision will allow persons with

disabilities to maximize their independence and enhance their well-being through access to required supports and the elimination of barriers that prevent their full participation.[12]

In many ways *In Unison* captured the approach to disability promoted in the disability movement, recognizing that disability is created by society and therefore requires actions by governments and all parts of society to remove stigma and ensure inclusion:

Most persons with disabilities no longer are seen or see themselves as dependent individuals with no ability to control their lives. They no longer are considered permanently unemployable or unable to contribute to society. Indeed, persons with disabilities contribute to Canadian society through art, culture, sports, political, voluntary and community activities, and other activities, which are not solely economic. These realities must be reflected in legislation, public policy and programs.

This vision was to be implemented in three key areas: disability supports, employment and income. The capturing of this vision by all levels of government was a significant step forward in the pursuit of disability rights.

In Unison came at the end of two decades of a lack of forward movement on disability policy. One prominent academic, Michael Prince, writing on disability policy in the era between 1981 and 2001, calls it the "déjà vu discourse of disability." He argues that the impotence of policy action arises from "the official declaration of plans and promises by governments and other public authorities, followed by external reviews of the record, and then official responses with a reiteration of previously stated plans and promises."[13] *In Unison* brought a vision that connected with the disability movement and coordinated governmental action around priority areas. But the question remains: was there significant policy action on disability rights in the following decade in response to this vision? In addition, has the more focused disability movement agenda since 2003 brought with it any momentum?

Disability Rights Policy in the 2000s

Since the early 2000s, the policy context related to disability has changed in terms of both key policies and where they are addressed. There has been a growth, as noted above, in the number of disability policy offices within governments, but the federal/provincial/territorial discussions around disability have been relatively infertile since the mid-2000s. The structure of funding for labour market agreements between the federal and provincial governments has become bilateral, with funds transferred by the federal government and a variety of actions taken and reports made by the provincial governments.[14] The provincial programs vary widely. As discussed in Chapter 3, there have been some gains in the employment of people with disabilities in the latter half of the 2000s, but it is unclear whether those have been lost with the recession of 2008–09.

The real shift in policy has been an increased focus, especially by the federal government, towards implementing tax measures for individuals with disabilities. The Registered Disability Savings Plan (RDSP) is the most significant initiative. It came as a response to the recommendations of the 2004 Technical Advisory Committee on Taxation.[15] The RDSP allows people to put aside money, tax free, with some matching funds from the federal government, for use at a later time by a family member with disabilities. The families of people with intellectual disabilities particularly championed this initiative as they realized their adult children might not have family support after their parents died. In addition, the Child Disability Benefit was created for parents who are caring for children with disabilities. It is a supplement to the Canada Child Tax Benefit.

The disability advocacy organizations have accepted tax as a policy direction, even though it is not their preferred means for achieving equality. The tax policy changes made in the late 2000s primarily assist persons who already have an income or, in the case of the RDSP, families with means. Recognizing that many people with disabilities do not have a source of income other than social assistance or other government programs, the disability advocacy organizations have argued for a refundable disability tax credit.[16]

Several provincial governments created disability supports programs in the years following the social union framework discussions. In 2001, Prince Edward Island took the lead and separated the provision of disability supports from income provision. This means that in P.E.I. it is possible for people with disabilities to receive the technical or social supports they need, like a wheelchair or assistance taking a bath, regardless of whether or not they receive income assistance.[17] New Brunswick followed a similar path in creating a personalized and flexible disability supports program without income support. Other provinces, including Saskatchewan, British Columbia and Ontario, have focused on creating or maintaining a disability income support program. The Canadian landscape for disability-related supports and income is an uneven patchwork of programs and services despite the *In Unison* framework and advocacy of disability organizations. This means real disparities in access to services and inclusion in society for people with disabilities across provinces. A 2006 Statistics Canada survey notes that people who need assistive devices are most likely to get these through publicly funded programs in Alberta, Quebec and the Territories, and least likely to receive public funding for devices in British Columbia. In Manitoba, the provincial government covers the costs of wheelchairs and their maintenance for people who live in the community, and not in an institutional setting. As well, if you move from the province, you must return your wheelchair. These disparities mean that people with disabilities are not able to move between provinces with any assurance of similar supports.

Aboriginal People with Disabilities

The variations across Canada and the gaps resulting from different governmental responsibilities are intensified for Aboriginal people with disabilities. First Nations, Metis and Inuit people with disabilities experience greater complexity as a result of the intersection of their Aboriginality and disability. The historical responsibility of the federal government for Aboriginal peoples and the desire for and implementation of self-government create a jurisdictional nightmare. This has led to significant exclusion and even death for some Aboriginal people with disabilities.

Yet in many Aboriginal cultures there is no word for disability and the cultural tradition is to include everyone in the community for what they bring:

> In Cree the word *kakanatisichek* means "the gifted ones, the special people." According to a traditional Cree woman disability is understood in a unique way within her culture: "There is no word in our language for disability, impairment or abnormality, but again this is only what I know for my community. The Creator put these people here for a purpose so that we will learn from them; they are our teachers. No one is considered abnormal in our culture." A traditional Oji-Cree woman suggests that the word for disability in her language is a "general term, never used to refer to another person. Rather the term is used to refer to a generalized condition needing acceptance, rather than needing further defining, classification or treatment."[18]

This approach is in significant contrast with how most Canadians understand disability.

Aboriginal people experience a higher incidence of impairment — between two to three times the rate in the non-Aboriginal population. This may be related to the predominance of chronic illnesses like diabetes, the barriers to access to health care, the systemic racism

Aboriginal people face and poverty both on and off First Nations communities. Alongside that increased presence of impairment and chronic illness is poverty. Rates of low income are twice as high among Aboriginal people with disabilities compared with non-Aboriginal people with disabilities — 38 percent compared to 19.5 percent.[19] So put simply, if you are Aboriginal in Canada, you are more likely to experience impairment and the barriers associated with that, and you are more likely to be poor than most disabled people.

Yet the complex story for Aboriginal people with disabilities does not end there. These issues have been recognized in public reports for more than thirty years with little forward movement in addressing them. The multiple reports on people with disabilities since the early 1980s have identified the situation of Aboriginal people as unique, the need for action urgent, and the jurisdictional complexities immense. It took the death of a small boy named Jordan River Anderson to put a leak in the jurisdictional logjam.

The complex interplay of governments and responsibilities is the result of the historical and constitutional responsibilities of the federal government for Aboriginal peoples. Yet the Charter of Rights and Freedoms also includes Aboriginal rights, which has led to the settling of some land claims and the devolution of responsibilities to Aboriginal governments.

Aboriginal people with disabilities who live outside First Nations communities can access the provincial services where they live. Yet on First Nations communities there are few community-based services, and much of the federally provided funds go to transporting people to services outside of the community: "The majority of the First Nations and Inuit Health Branch budget (58 of 110 million dollar budget in 2004) is currently spent transporting people out of the community to provincially funded health services as opposed to supporting community based, community defined supports and services."[20] This leads to situations like Jordan's, where people with disabilities are not able to be in their own homes because they need services that are not available in the community.

Jordan River Anderson

Jordan River Anderson of Norway House Cree Nation was born in October 1999 with multiple impairments. He was ready to go home from hospital when he was two years old but he went on to spend over two years unnecessarily in hospital as the Province of Manitoba and the Government of Canada could not agree on who should pay for his at home care. Jordan died at age 5 on February 2, 2005, before he could go home. As Cindy Blackstock of the First Nations Child and Family Caring Society said "Jordan could not talk, yet people around the world heard his message. Jordan could not breathe on his own and yet he has given the breath of life to other children. Jordan could not walk but he has taken steps that governments are now just learning to follow." Jordan's short life has come to symbolize one significant situation of Aboriginal people with disabilities in Canada.

Source: <http://www.fncfcs.com/jordans-principle>.

Jordan's case illustrates the greater complexities of federal-provincial funding arrangements. "Shortly after Jordan's second birthday, doctors said he could go to a family home. This decision should have been a time of celebration but for federal and provincial governments it was a time to begin arguing over which department would pay for Jordan's at home care. The jurisdictional dispute would last over two years during which time Jordan remained unnecessarily in hospital. The costs they argued over ranged from some higher cost items such as renovations to the home for a wheelchair ramp to low cost items such as showerheads."[21] From Jordan's death in hospital has come a movement to adopt "Jordan's Principle." It calls for the government of first contact to pay for the services and treatment and then seek reimbursement afterwards. As of 2011, British Columbia, Saskatchewan and Manitoba have committed to implement it, but no governments have implemented it in whole.

While Jordan's Principle has been embraced by many, Don Shackel, who works in First Nations communities and is completing a Ph.D. in inclusive special education, argues that Jordan's Principle may hurt as much as it helps. First, it only addresses jurisdictional conflicts. "Factors such as a lack of service infrastructures, or the isolated nature of some communities… non-targeting of allocated funds at the community level, may also impact the lack of access to services and supports."[22] Second, Jordan's Principle is based in a medical approach rather than a social model of disability and thus focuses attention to those with medically complex needs at the expense of those with less complex needs, but who also require disability-related supports, like American Sign Language (ASL) interpretation. Shackel also argues that Jordan's Principle situates disability supports in the child welfare system, making it a child protection issue, rather than addressing it as a life-long need, with differing supports required from birth to death. Finally, the approach taken in Jordan's Principle leads to a case-by-case resolution of jurisdictional conflicts rather than a cohesive set of disability supports for Aboriginal people.

An additional part of the story of Aboriginal people with disabilities is the legacy of residential schools. Being required to leave home for extended periods of time for services reminds many people of leaving their communities for residential schools where they experienced physical, sexual and cultural abuse. Because of the possibilities of harm and the lack of family support when people leave their community, many families want those who require services to remain. This can be seen as resilience — drawing on the strengths of communities and traditional ways in order to meet challenges. One family member in Manitoba gave their reasons:

> They said we should send him out to that school (the Manitoba School for the Deaf). We have been there twice. It is hard to send your child into the outside by himself especially when he has a medical problem. He belongs with his people, his family. We will lose him if he is over there. He belongs in his community. I want him here. When my dad was sick he said, "Do not send him out. Let him stay

here and learn the traditional way of our people. Do not let him go to the city or he will get killed."[23]

The interplay of Aboriginal rights and disability rights as well as culture shape the lives and experiences of Aboriginal people with disabilities in Canada. Many times, the experiences are of exclusion, poverty and inappropriate and insufficient services and supports. The stories of people like Jordan River Anderson remind disability advocates and policy-makers of the human consequences of the lack of disability and Aboriginal rights and the importance of honouring the strengths of Aboriginal cultures.

One Step Forward...?

In the past thirty years Canada saw increasing and coordinated advocacy by people with disabilities, many public reports outlining issues and barriers to people with disabilities, a broad policy framework that identifies key directions for action and recognition of the unique situation for Aboriginal people with disabilities. These people and policies begin with a commitment to the rights of people with disabilities. Yet what happens when people with disabilities fall through the cracks of existing rights and policies?

2. WHEN PEOPLE WITH DISABILITIES FALL THROUGH THE CRACKS

Many stories about people with disabilities are not easy either to write or to read. Each of the stories below is about a person who faced barriers as a result of disability but the rights and services they were eligible to receive were not there. They all died. Their stories illustrate how disability is viewed by Canadian society and remind us of the more subtle ways that we include and exclude people with disabilities. These painful stories of loss and death may be a beginning to understanding and identifying new ways to include and appreciate the diversity of Canadians.

Brian Sinclair

On September 21, 2008, in the emergency room of the Winnipeg Health Sciences Centre, Brian Sinclair died. He had been waiting for thirty-four hours for treatment for a bladder infection. The chief medical examiner ruled that his death could have been prevented with a change of catheter and antibiotics. As of October 2011, three years later, a public inquest into his death has not been held.

Brian Sinclair was Aboriginal, forty-five years old, a wheelchair user; his two legs had been amputated, he had communications barriers, and he was homeless.

As time goes on, the stakes get higher for everyone. Initially, hospital staff and others, including senior officials in the Winnipeg Regional Health Authority (WRHA), the minister of health, and the premier, said that Brian Sinclair had not seen a triage nurse to assess his condition and get him in the queue for treatment.

After security tapes were reviewed, the story changed, and it was agreed that Brian had spoken with someone at triage. In February 2009, the chief medical officer revealed that Brian Sinclair had been vomiting in the emergency room while security staff tried unsuccessfully to get the triage staff to pay attention to him. He called for a public inquest in to Brian Sinclair's death, but it has not yet been held.

In September 2010, the family of Brian Sinclair filed a civil lawsuit against the WRHA, the Manitoba government and the hospital staff on duty. In October 2010, the Winnipeg Police launched a criminal investigation into the circumstances of Brian Sinclair's death. The public inquest has been delayed until the criminal investigation is complete. In February 2011, the Office of the Manitoba Ombudsman ruled that the Sinclair family and their legal counsel could not have access to the videotapes and WRHA records related to Brian Sinclair's death until the public inquest is held.

The Sinclair family has raised their concerns with United Nations Special Rapporteurs and called for both a public inquest and a more general public inquiry related to Aboriginal health care in Manitoba.

Ashley Smith

On October 19, 2007, nineteen-year-old Ashley Smith died from asphyxiation in her cell at Grand Valley Institution for Women in Kitchener, Ontario. The correctional investigator ruled that Ashley Smith's death was preventable. Ashley Smith tied a ligature around her neck. The report says that video illustrates that correctional staff failed to respond immediately to this emergency and watched her die.

Ashley Smith was an Aboriginal woman from Moncton, New Brunswick. She lived with mental health disabilities from age thirteen and exhibited "challenging" behaviours that meant she was in and out of school. As journalist Christie Blatchford tells, Ashley Smith was in jail not because she was a hardened criminal but because she was "a mentally disturbed girl whose worst crimes, if they can even be so labelled, were pulling fire alarms, pelting a mailman with apples and making harassing phone calls."[1]

In the last year of her life, she was moved seventeen times, primarily between different correctional institutions. Her life in prison, both in New Brunswick as a juvenile, and in many provinces as an adult, has been the subject of multiple reports and a high profile investigative television program on CBC's *The Fifth Estate*. The correctional investigator found that Ashley Smith had severely limited access to appropriate mental health support and received only cursory mental health assessment, care and treatment. His report concluded:

> Ms. Smith had mental health issues which had been aggravated by years of isolation in secure provincial youth facilities. Nevertheless, the Correctional Service placed Ms. Smith on administrative segregation status — under a highly restrictive, and at times, inhumane regime — and maintained her on this status for her entire period of federal custody....
>
> The federal/provincial health care and correctional systems collectively failed to provide Ms. Smith with the appropriate care, treatment and support she desperately required. The tragic death of Ms. Smith not only speaks to breakdowns within federal corrections, but also to a lack of coordination and cohesiveness among federal/provincial/territorial mental health and correctional systems.[2]

Ashley Smith's family launched a lawsuit against the federal government in October 2009 and settled it in May 2011. A coroner's inquest into her death was not completed as of October 2011.

Cory Moar

On December 11, 1998, Cory Moar died in Winnipeg, not of the injuries he came into the hospital with this time, but of the accumulation of beatings and injuries that he had sustained over the previous years.

Cory Moar was twenty-nine years old. He had hearing loss and was labelled mildly intellectually impaired. He lived with his brother and family. Cory Moar received disability services related to employment, independent living and social assistance. He was not eligible for protection under the *Vulnerable Persons Living with a Mental Disability Act* because his I.Q. scores were not low enough. He continued to live in a home where his brother and a youth beat him with a car jack and two-by-fours. Cory Moar did not disclose that he was being abused.

Associate Chief Justice Oliphant, at the adult criminal trial related to Cory Moar's death, called for an inquiry

> into the shocking death of a mentally disabled man who was kept prisoner in his own home.... I don't understand why warning flags didn't go off, and why someone didn't do something. Perhaps had someone cared to pay attention to Cory Moar and his plight, he wouldn't be dead.
>
> This is a man who has slipped through the cracks. For sure, this should not have happened. Society in general should feel ashamed.[3]

In the inquest report into Cory Moar's death, Judge Kopstein identified several gaps in the support services that contributed to Cory Moar falling through the cracks. There was little knowledge about or training of service providers to identify and report abuse of people with disabilities. There was no shelter to which people with disabilities could go if they didn't fit the criteria for existing shelters. There was a lack of public information and resources about the right not to be abused and what to do in cases of abuse.

Tracy Latimer

On October 23, 1993, Tracy Latimer was murdered by her father, Robert Latimer, on the family farm in Wilkie, Saskatchewan. While the family was in church on a Sunday, he put Tracy in the cab of his pickup truck, inserted a hose from the exhaust pipe into the cab and left her to die of carbon monoxide poisoning.

Tracy Latimer was born on November 23, 1980. She was the eldest of four children. She had cerebral palsy and was a wheelchair user. Tracy attended a developmental program at the same school as her siblings and travelled on a school bus with the other students. Her mother's journal notes that she was a happy child and enjoyed music and being with her family. Even though doctors recommended a feeding tube, Tracy's parents chose not to have that support. Tracy Latimer had multiple surgeries and was described as in pain by her mother. As the Supreme Court noted, Tracy Latimer had a serious disability but was not terminally ill.[4] In October 1993, the physician recommended another surgery for her hip. Shortly after that, her father decided to end her life.

Robert Latimer was convicted of second-degree murder and sentenced to ten years in prison without parole. He appealed his sentence to both the Saskatchewan Court of Appeal and the Supreme Court of Canada. In 2001, the Supreme Court upheld the conviction and his sentence. On December 6, 2010, after serving ten years in prison, Robert Latimer was granted full parole. As recently as March 2011, in a television interview on *Canada AM*, Robert Latimer expressed no regret for his decision to end Tracy's life.[5] Robert Latimer's actions have galvanized national discussions about the right to murder those believed to be suffering.

What Do Their Stories Tell Us?

The deaths of these four people tell us much about how people with disabilities are viewed in Canada. Disabled people are set aside by neglect, failure to recognize and address harm or abuse, and acts of murder that are seen to be justified by assertions of compassion. People with disabilities are implicitly and explicitly told that they are not worthy, or of enough value, to receive human rights and related protections because they are, or cause, too much trouble or require too many resources. Finally, we are told through these stories that it is better to be dead, or not to be born, than to live with disability. In these ways, the exclusion and marginalization of people with disabilities shifts from benign indifference, or invisibility, to neglect, acts of abuse and murder.

Set Aside and Invisible

Brian Sinclair was literally set aside and out of view of those providing public health care services. We don't yet know why or how this happened. What we do know is that his invisibility, in the corner of the emergency room, led to his neglect and finally death. His death is a graphic example of what happens when people with disabilities are set aside and neglected, out of the public view.

Unfortunately, many people with disabilities have been and continue to be set aside in public institutions, including long-term care homes and long-standing institutions. Despite recent closures of institutions in Ontario, hundreds of people with disabilities continue to live at large and long-established institutions in Alberta, Saskatchewan and Manitoba. A class action lawsuit has been brought by a thousand former residents of Huronia Regional Centre in Ontario and their families for abuse. The suit alleges "that the Province's failure to care for and protect residents resulted in loss or injury suffered by them, including psychological trauma, pain and suffering, loss of enjoyment of life, and exacerbation of existing mental disabilities."[6] A class action suit was filed by survivors of the Woodlands School in British Columbia and settled in 2010. In Nova Scotia, forty-nine cases of abuse were uncovered in residential centres between October 2007 and July 2009. These included a case where staff placed a bar of soap in a resident's mouth and one where a staff member grabbed a resident by the leg and pulled her down a hallway.[7]

Many of those who have lived in institutions all of their lives are people with intellectual impairments or mental illness. They were often placed there as children when their families were unable to cope with the extra demands resulting from their impairments. These families chose a different route than Robert Latimer, but their choices have not been without significant and long-lasting emotional and physical scars to all the individuals involved.

Equally troubling is the use of institutions to address the care needs of younger people with brain injuries, strokes or deteriorating conditions like multiple sclerosis or ALS. As their conditions worsen, these individuals are often placed in long-term nursing homes meant for seniors. In a 2004 *Globe and Mail* report, Lisa Priest found that at least 8560 people under the age of sixty-five lived in nursing homes across Canada. "Younger disabled adults usually arrive in nursing homes after they have exhausted all other routes, fallen on hard times, lost family support or suffered an illness that makes it impossible to obtain enough services to live independently."[8] The lack of appropriate disability supports and insufficient community-based care often leads to institutionalization for these younger people with disabilities.

Many people with disabilities in nursing homes feel out of place after having lived their lives in the community. For some it feels inappropriate. Donna Froese says, "It's not where I should be. It feels degrading."[9] Madeleine Vallée tells her story of shifting from a vibrant and interesting life with friends and a fun social life to what she has now.

> I don't sleep much. I spend much of my days listening to radio and to audio books. I entertain the odd visitor…. I'm

mostly the silent observer here, trying not to rock the boat but trying to get needs met at the same time.

Like the weekly bath... Being ministered to by a near-stranger is something I may never get used to. When you become a resident in a nursing home, you leave your privacy and dignity at the door.[10]

Being set aside in a nursing home, as in the earlier institutions, can harm or sever ties with family and friends. Being among people with dementia and of a very different age group, as well as in settings created for seniors, can lead to isolation, boredom and depression. Ultimately, it can rob people of meaning and purpose and, with it, the will to live.

Living independently, with sufficient disability supports, allows many people with disabilities to be part of and contribute to their communities. Justin Clark was one of the pioneers of living independently in the community. In 1981, against the wishes of his parents who wanted to have him declared mentally incompetent, he fought for and won the right to make decisions about his own life and leave the institution in which he had lived for sixteen years. He continues to live in the community, working as a computer consultant.[11]

Unworthy of Rights and Protections

Ashley Smith was told repeatedly that she was too much trouble, too demanding and causing too much stress on the system and the workers. Cory Moar was beaten repeatedly. He tried to live independently but did not succeed. In the final days of his life, when his injuries became too visible, Cory Moar was forced to live in the basement.

Both appear to have received the message from those around them that they were not worthy or valued. Cory Moar made no claim for his right not to be abused or for protection from his abusers. Despite the long-established messages that she was too much for the corrections system, Ashley Smith reached out to the Elizabeth

Fry Society and asked for help. She outlined what she believed were improper treatments, including assaults from the staff, inadequate living conditions, lack of psychiatric care and frequent segregation and transfers. She gave Kim Pate of the Elizabeth Fry Society permission to act on her behalf in getting her personal records. This act of reaching out meant that Ashley Smith's story has become public and caused the system and the broader public to recognize the gaps and abuse that happened in her case.

For Cory Moar, support from the broader community of people with disabilities came only after his death. A coalition of disability advocacy groups attended his inquest and provided evidence of issues his death raised for people with disabilities. The local Association for Community Living held vigils in Cory Moar's name to raise awareness of violence against disabled people. The Allan Simpson Memorial Fund sponsored a community strategy meeting addressing violence and abuse against people with disabilities.

The CCD says in its 2002–03 annual report that it became involved in the Cory Moar inquest to ensure that the judge had the benefit of a disability rights framework to develop recommendations that would support the disability rights and independent living aspirations of people with disabilities. "In cases of horrific violence and abuse, there is always the danger that people who are unfamiliar with the social history of people with disabilities will fall back on the medical model approaches to disabilities, such as institutionalization, that purport to keep people with disabilities safe, rather than strive to devise new solutions that promote full citizenship."[12] Some of these new solutions involve different ways of thinking about legal competency and decision-making capacity, including supported decision-making, discussed in Chapter 4. The UNCRPD recognizes that some people require assistance to exercise their capacity to make decisions and offers some ideas about how to develop and use support networks that enhance a person's capacity to make decisions, rather than a substitute who makes decisions for the person.[13]

Better Dead than Disabled

In the 1994 trial of Robert Latimer, Tracy's mother, Laura, testified that Tracy's birth was much sadder than her death. Laura Latimer believed they had lost Tracy when she was born. These sentiments reflect a much broader perception of disability by Canadians — that it is better to be dead than to live with disabilities. In her death, Tracy Latimer reminds us that these attitudes and beliefs are not abstract but can have life-and-death consequences for people, including people in vulnerable circumstances like Tracy Latimer.

Robert Latimer is not unique in his actions, but he is the most high profile and is without remorse. Many Canadians believe that it is better to end the suffering of people who are in pain, by euthanasia or assisted suicide, and support the actions of Robert Latimer. Indeed in the late 1990s, Heidi Janz, a disability studies scholar and playwright, argued that public perceptions and the media portrayals of Robert Latimer had a direct impact on the proceedings of his cases. Tracy Latimer and her severe disability were consistently portrayed as a burden to herself and her family.

> When this portrayal of Tracy is contrasted with the typical depiction of Robert Latimer as a devoted parent and a well-liked, well-respected member of the community, it becomes painfully evident that the mass media is at once mirroring and perpetuating the common public perception of people with severe disabilities as somehow less-than-human beings condemned to a burdensome, pain-filled existence. The lives of people with severe disabilities are thus being subtly but systematically devalued by our society.[14]

Many Canadians believe that assisted suicide and euthanasia are justified in cases like Tracy Latimer and where it is believed the person lives with significant pain and suffering. A life that appears to be dependent on others, limited in mobility, without what we think of as "normal" activity is not a valued life, or one that we would want.

Perceptions of suffering and the desire to end it have led to a flourishing public debate on assisted suicide and euthanasia. Provincial and federal legislators have contributed through reports, committee hearings and private members' bills. Disability groups argue that people with disabilities are at great risk in situations where euthanasia or assisted suicide is legalized. Supporters of assisted suicide call for the right to choose when to die for those whose lives are difficult to bear.

Popular culture perpetuates the link between disability, suffering and ending life by euthanasia or assisted suicide. Mainstream Hollywood movies, like the 2004 Academy Award winner *Million Dollar Baby,* suggest that disability is too difficult to bear both for the individual and for those around him or her and that both assisted suicide and euthanasia are appropriate responses. In *Million Dollar Baby*, Maggie, who trains to become a boxer with a chance at a championship fight, is attacked and receives a career-ending spinal cord injury. The movie faces the question of whether her life is worth saving or ending. She asks for help in ending her life from her trainer and in the end he agrees to do it. As several disability researchers illustrate, negative images of disability fill the movie and could easily lead those watching to concur that death was the only solution for Maggie:

> After her operation, Maggie's "deterioration" is plainly evident. She is never out of bed or dressed. She never smiles. Her hair is loose and tangled. Gone are the fancy braids of the beloved fighter. Her eyes are sunken, ringed in black. Her lips are chapped. Her skin looks white and pasty. In short, she is the image of death. Watching the film, we share her despondency. She can no longer fight. She has lost the will to live. Who would want to live a life of paralysis, relying on a respirator to take a breath? Of course she wants to die, we empathize. Who wouldn't, in her situation? Life has nothing to offer her and she is competent to make the decision

to die. If she were able, she could kill herself, no questions asked. Frankie is right to help her die because Maggie feels worthless and is convinced she has nothing to live for.[15]

In contrast to this popular portrayal of the horror of living with disability, there are many stories from people with disabilities who have and continue to lead a good life until the end. They don't cover up the complexities of living with impairments, accommodations and the barriers of a society geared to able-bodied people. But they reject the devaluation and worthlessness projected in the popular portrayals. Rather, they talk of being able to contribute, using their abilities and being liberated by technologies including ventilators. One of the most eloquent spokespeople for this perspective is a judge in Ontario, Sam Filer, who lived for nineteen years with ALS until his death at seventy-one years old (in a house fire) in 2007.

> In my case, it's likely that my condition and the limitations it imposes on me would be found on most lists of 10 top things that make for a life lacking in quality. Let me assure you: I am not confined to a wheelchair, I am mobilized by one. I am not ventilator-dependent, I am a happy consumer of a lung-expanding, breath-giving device which allows me to continue doing the things I love. It has given me, and us, a degree of independence and a second chance at life, that we would otherwise not have had.

> The doctors told me that ALS is a virtual death sentence. But I am not "dying from" a life-threatening disease — I am "living with" a life-enhancing condition.

> Far from rendering me "disabled," the ventilator, the wheelchair, the computer, have empowered me, to a level of ability not previously considered, given the constraints imposed by ALS. They allow me to maximize my abilities, rather than focus on my disabilities.[16]

As Sam Filer and others remind us, living with disabilities, as life in general, is about finding meaning and purpose and connecting through relationships. It is about the enjoyment of music and family that Tracy Latimer experienced. And for those who provide support and care, it is about ensuring respect and dignity to those who receive that care and support. It is about honouring the diverse experiences of life, even those that are at times difficult and are not ones we would chose. It is not about "dying from" but rather *living with* disability.

3. DISABILITY RIGHTS AND KEY AREAS OF CANADIAN SOCIETY

Some may suggest that the four stories told in Chapter 2 are the exception, not the rule, of living with disabilities in Canada. Indeed, Sam Filer argued that with appropriate disability supports, he was able to live a good, if challenging, life with ALS. What are the experiences of people with disabilities in achieving disability rights? Five keys areas of access and inclusion — education, employment, transportation, telecommunications and health care — are necessary building blocks for full inclusion and participation in Canadian society. Yet despite some strong disability rights protections, women and men with disabilities are among the most poor, excluded and disenfranchised of Canadians. As Sam Filer said, there are dramatic circumstances in the lives of people with disabilities, but they also live rich and full lives despite obstacles. These contrasts can propel us to thinking and acting to identify and implement solutions that address these disparities.

Education

One of the initial building blocks to inclusion in Canadian society is having access to education. This covers early childhood education and childcare, education in primary, middle and secondary schools, postsecondary education and lifelong learning. To what extent are children and adults with disabilities included in each of these areas of education?

Childcare

Childcare is an important part of the lives of many Canadian parents and critical for those in the labour force. For parents of children with disabilities, childcare is also important, but it must meet the unique needs of their children. In 2006, almost one-third of parents of children with disabilities used some form of childcare, whether it was a daycare centre, care in their own or another's home, nursery school or before- and after-school care.[1] For parents of children with complex impairments the need for childcare was especially significant. Over 90 percent of parents of children with disabilities said that it was essential for the staff to be able to address the special needs of their child and that the facility was physically accessible. More than one in five parents of children with disabilities have been refused childcare as a result of their child's disabilities (see Chart 1), and this increased for children with more complex impairments, with almost one-third of their parents refused service.

As the Childcare Advocacy Association of Canada argues, inclusion in childcare is more than simply being able to access childcare:

> Simply put, childcare inclusion means that all children can attend and benefit from the same child care programs. It means that children with disabilities go to the same programs they would attend if they did not have a disability. Inclusion means all children, not just those who are easy and/or less expensive to include. All means all. For children with disabilities, this means that the necessary supports of training, equipment, physical modifications and extra staffing are available to all programs, at no extra cost to parents or to the individual programs. The principle of inclusion goes beyond the notion of physical integration and fully

Chart 1: Between 10 percent and 25 percent of Canadian parents of disabled children report that a program or service refused to provide childcare.

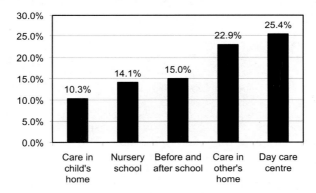

Source: Statistics Canada. 2008. *Participation and Activity Limitation Survey 2006: Families of Children with Disabilities in Canada.* Ottawa: Ministry of Industry.

incorporates basic values that promote and advance participation, friendship and a celebration of diversity. Children with all disabilities are active participants, not just observers on the sidelines.[2]

When 20 to 30 percent of parents are refused childcare for their child with disabilities, inclusion is not happening.

Education for Students with Disabilities

Once children are ready for school, access and inclusion can continue to be a problem for children with disabilities. Canada has a universal education policy, yet many children with disabilities are not getting the education they need. Either they cannot access special education or they are unable to get the supports they need for education. As Human Resources and Skills Development Canada (HRSDC) reports, although most children with disabilities attend school, 4,000 Canadian children with disabilities do not go to any school, because there is either no school or insufficient supports.[3]

Rebecca Beayni

Rebecca has been blessed ironically, with Cerebral Palsy, and an intellectual disability which makes her dependent on others for almost everything. Despite this, Rebecca had led and continues to lead a favoured life where she is an integral, functional, and impactful member of her society. She represents persons with disabilities who demand to invoke their rights as citizens to be seen, heard, and allowed to make meaningful contributions to the community. Usually, when people see Rebecca, they do not initially see her as being able to share and contribute. It is not her physical limitations but rather an attitude of unwillingness to see beyond them, that can bar her from becoming a full citizen.

A part of being a whole society or a democratic society, is making certain ALL voices are heard, and decisions are made for the common good. However, some of our society's most vulnerable citizens are ignored. Rebecca forces people to slow down to communicate with her and this is a gift to the world… slowing people down to the point where they have to listen to those, otherwise ignored, voices. This guides us in the direction of a good society; which is measured by how people treat, listen deeply to, empathize and interact with its most vulnerable members.

Rebecca's school and later work experience is a testament to how one person can change the entire culture that exists around them. Teachers, administrators, fellow students, and co-workers always say that Rebecca's mere presence changes the very fabric of their relationships, making them more collaborative, more compassionate, and more intuitive to strategies that advantage all persons.

Rebecca was fully included and integrated into the regular classroom since elementary school and she has had wonderful teachers who planned creatively and effectively to cater to her learning needs. Part of this was having Rebecca's classmates play critical roles in assisting her and helping her teachers to create accommodations that would be to her benefit as well. Not only did these youngsters learn the importance of responsibility for others, task commitment and community building, they also gained from an educational perspective as well; since teaching strategies used to assist Rebecca helped all levels of learners. I remember when Rebecca was in the eighth grade, she was out in the school yard and some of the boys in her class were "skipping" with her. She has always loved to watch children skip so her classmates, when they were younger figured that she could skip too if they just turned the ropes back and forth over her head as she sat in her wheel chair. It was amazing to see that even in grade 8 when 14 year old boys are trying to assert themselves in the stereotypical ways of young men, that they exhibited such tenderness towards their friend's desire to play with them.

Source: Rebecca Beayni. 2005. "Rebecca's presentation to the United Nations Ad Hoc Committee on the Rights and Dignity of Persons with Disabilities," August 3, 2005. <http://rebeccabeayni.com/AboutMe_PresentationtoUnitedNations.html>. Used with permission.

In 2006, Statistics Canada documented the situation of children with disabilities in special education. More than 40 percent of children with disabilities between the ages of five and fourteen received some form of special education, whether through special classes in a regular school or in a special school.[4] Among the parents who believed their child required special education, more than 40 percent of their children were not receiving this. Almost one-half of the parents whose children received special education reported that they had had difficulties in getting this for their children.

In addition, many children with disabilities require specific aids or services to participate in school. These disability supports might be a ramp or railing to get into their classroom or the washroom, but they can also include teaching assistants, special software or computer equipment or attendant care. More than one in five students with disabilities did not have the disability supports they needed to get an education. Most parents (75 percent) said this was a result of a lack of funding within the school system.[5]

Barriers to education increased for students with disabilities between the ages of fifteen and nineteen. Only just over three-quarters of the youth with disabilities attended school.[6] The major reasons for their lack of completion include long absences because of their impairments and having to leave their communities in order to get education.

In 2008, the Council of Ministers of Education of Canada,

which is the national body coordinating policy on education in Canada, made the following commitment: "All children in our elementary to high school systems deserve teaching and learning opportunities that are inclusive and that provide them with world-class skills in literacy, numeracy, and science."[7] Inclusive education remains out of reach for many elementary, middle and high school students with disabilities. Their inclusion relies upon sufficient funds for disability supports and physically accessible buildings, adequate training and resources for teachers and curriculum that recognizes and values the experiences of people with disabilities.

Access to Postsecondary Education

There is widespread recognition that more education increases chances of employment and having an adequate income. Completion rates for high school are lower for people with disabilities than for people without disabilities in Canada. Based on 2006 data, Statistics Canada reported that 25.4 percent of working-age adults with disabilities had not received any certificate for school completion, compared to 13.5 percent of working-age adults without disabilities.[8]

A 2011 study by the Higher Education Quality Council of Ontario showed that students with disabilities make up 6 to 7 percent of students on college and university campuses in Canada.[9] Like all women, more women with disabilities are completing some postsecondary education. A higher proportion of students with disabilities are in college versus university education. But it is clear that people with disabilities are under-represented in postsecondary education in Canada. In addition, they face multiple barriers to accessing postsecondary education, including lack of physical access and appropriate disability supports as well as curriculum that can render them invisible.

The same 2011 study identifies some significant barriers, including the extra costs of equipment or resources related to obtaining education given their impairment. These direct costs may include sign language interpretation, special equipment, personal assistants and tutors. But the study also identified indirect costs for students with disabilities, including a longer time to complete their education, because of their impairments and/or external requirements about how many courses they can take as a student with disabilities.

One barrier not often discussed is the effect that the non-disabled perception of disability and people with disabilities can have on students with disabilities in achieving their postsecondary education. One-half of the 2011 study respondents identified societal attitudes about disability as a source of disability, with the statement, "If the attitudes of society were more open, I would not be considered as disabled."

In addition to barriers for people within postsecondary education, there are barriers for many people with disabilities even to begin college or university. People with intellectual disabilities are often prevented from entering because of the perception that they are not intellectually able to undertake this level of education. Some universities in Canada have introduced programs to enable people with intellectual disabilities to audit, with supports, postsecondary courses.

Inclusion in postsecondary education for students with disabilities is an ongoing struggle, with additional costs for disability supports, insufficient funding for disability services and accommodations, attitudes of many that restrict people with disabilities from achieving what they can and lack of recognition of the unique challenges and obstacles that students with disabilities face.

Lifelong Learning and People with Disabilities

Ongoing education and learning is essential for everyone, whether to get a job or for career advancement, or for personal growth and social connections. As with other areas of education, the barriers to lifelong learning often include lack of access to disability supports, attitudes about capacity or abilities and the costs in relation to income. In addition, some of the issues raised previously around the longer time it often takes students with disabilities to complete

Marie-Eve Veilleux

Disability in Science: A Student's Success

Marie-Eve Veilleux was a speaker at the NEADS [National Educational Association for Disabled Students] conference in Ottawa in November 2008. She told delegates in the workshop presentation that when she was 18 months old, she was diagnosed with a severe form of arthritis that caused extensive mobility problems and progressively destroyed her knees, hips, wrists, and fingers. This made writing and carrying books extremely painful, and her academic life even more difficult. The disease attacked all her joints. After many painful surgeries, Veilleux regained the use of her legs, "but it is still hard to walk," she said.

Veilleux, who holds a Bachelor's degree in Microbiology and Immunology, began studying at McGill University out of pure interest in learning more about her condition, although she knew she would never be able to work in a lab. Pursuing a science degree — which involves working in labs, writing papers, and conducting research — was not the easiest choice. She was at the conference to prove that it was possible, "because I did it," said Veilleux.

She explained that she collaborated with the Office for Students with Disabilities at McGill to find creative ways to meet her degree require-ments. Her strategy was to involve people every step of the way. Common accommodations were available to her from the very beginning, for which Veilleux was grateful. However, she said, she wished to elaborate on some of the difficulties that students with disabilities face in science programs involving laboratory work.

The visually impaired are particularly challenged when asked to use microscopes to identify the color of bacteria, for example. Veilleux said she was unable to perform some of the most elementary tasks, such as handling a pipette or doing up the buttons of her lab coat. She was provided with a personal attendant whose duty was to do what Veilleux could not — tie her hair, put on her gloves, perform her practical exams. Veilleux would analyze the results and answer the questions.

This was not the best solution, she admitted. It was uncomfortable to continually ask someone to do things for her. So the following year, instead of being provided with an attendant, Veilleux was put in a team of three students instead of the usual two. In this way, while two students did lab work, Veilleux watched and wrote down data. Her practical exam was switched to a written exam. She would describe the experiments and the results and write a conclusion. This new approach worked. It eliminated her anxiety and stress, thus improving her academic performance.

Veilleux encouraged students with disabilities to collaborate with university staff to find appropriate arrangements and to talk to professors directly, rather than involve a greater number of people. "Sometimes it is better," she said. "Sometimes, you just don't have the energy."

When it comes to requesting and getting accommodations, Veilleux said, there are no right or wrong answers. Students must find their own way.

The heavy course load in science is also a problem, Veilleux said. Students who are already stressed with coping with a disability could find the stress of theoretical courses overwhelming. Veilleux discovered after starting the program that she could become a part-time student, which markedly improved her grades and her quality of life. Veilleux encouraged students with low energy levels to consider becoming part-time students and to apply for scholarships. She said policies that award scholarships to full-time students only — which she is still fighting — should not prevent anyone from applying.

After completing her science degree, Veilleux learned that finding a job was not easy. Most advanced career paths that suited her physical limitations did not interest her. It was then that she discovered her passion and talent for language and became a scientific translator. Her academic goal for 2009 is to pursue a Master's in Epidemiology, a post-graduate science program that involves statistics, not labs. Veilleux said her greatest pride was having proven all naysayers wrong. She said she hoped her example would encourage all persons with disabilities to apply to their program of choice.

Source: NEADS. n.d. "Marie-Eve Veilleux — Disability in Science: A Student's Success." <neads.ca/en/about/projects/stem/stem_profile_Veilleux.php>. Used with permission.

education have an impact in this area and are also true for many adult learners with disabilities.

Statistics Canada suggests that roughly one-quarter of employed people with disabilities have access to formal and informal workplace training. Of those who wanted to access training, cost was a barrier for 26 percent of them.[10]

In a 2008 community-based study on the needs of adult learners with disabilities, participants identified accessibility, financial issues and attitudes, including social stigma and a lack of knowledge about disability as barriers to learning.[11] They recommended that inclusive learning ensures secure funding so that persons with disabilities can be lifelong learners; accessible transportation and accessible buildings; multiple formats for learning and testing materials; peer support networks and services for adult learners with disabilities; and disability-awareness training for educators.

Inclusive Education and Disability Rights

At every stage of life, inclusive education in Canada remains illusive, with physical and attitudinal barriers, a lack of disability supports, additional costs for people with disabilities and invisibility in the content and structures of education. Despite these significant gaps in accessing education at every step, the Council of Ministers of Education of Canada does not address the situation of people with disabilities in its plan, *Learn Canada 2020*, which has as its vision "the provision of quality lifelong learning opportunities for all Canadians."

This omission may come in part from the 1997 decision of the Supreme Court of Canada on the inclusion of Emily Eaton, a disabled student, in her local school. The Ontario Court of Appeal had ruled in 1996 that "unless the parents of a child who has been identified as exceptional by reason of a physical or mental disability consent to the placement of that child in a segregated environment, the school board must provide a placement that is the least exclusionary from the mainstream and still reasonably capable of meeting the child's special needs."[12] The Supreme Court overturned that deci-

Including Disability in Curriculum

The Canadian Centre on Disability Studies created a toolkit for middle-school educators called *Disability, Development and Diversity: People with Disabilities in Canada and around the World*. The curriculum has been tested in two school divisions — one in Saskatchewan and the other in Manitoba, as well as in Uganda and the Ukraine. This Toolkit is designed for all teachers and all classrooms. This is not a special education resource. The Toolkit focuses about issues facing people with disabilities including: the language of disability, different ways of looking at and understanding disability, disability around the world, and disability in the media.

Source: <disabilitystudies.ca/ddd-home>.

sion saying that Emily Eaton should receive specialized education in a segregated setting despite the disability rights in the Charter of Rights and Freedoms.

Many have found this ruling inconsistent with disability rights. Dianne Pothier, a legal scholar, argues that the decision assumes a "separate but equal approach" to people with disabilities and perpetuates segregation and inferior status of people with disabilities.[13] She maintains that the disability rights in section 15 of the Charter demand integrated rather than segregated education for students with disabilities.

Despite the gaps in disability rights for inclusive education, educators have begun to include disability in the curriculum in K-12 and postsecondary schools. Disability studies based in a social model perspective is taught as a separate program at the undergraduate level in multiple programs in Canada, including University of Winnipeg, University of Windsor and Ryerson University. Graduate programs in disability studies are found at the University of Manitoba, York University, and University of Calgary.

The gaps in inclusive education reverberate through every area of life for people with disabilities, including their success in getting and retaining employment, although including disability studies at all levels of education has the possibility of positive transformation in perceptions of disability.

Employment

Employment has been long recognized as essential to the inclusion and full participation of people with disabilities in Canadian society. Yet despite long-standing program and policy efforts to increase the employment of people with disabilities, there remain significant differences between the employment, income and inclusion in the labour force of people with and without disabilities.

How do we make sense of the complex situation of people with disabilities in the labour force? Answers to three interconnected questions — Who is in the labour force? Who is unemployed? And who is not in the labour force and why? — help us understand the current situation for people with disabilities in Canada in relation to employment. They also illustrate the gaps in the employment and income of people with disabilities and the importance, but limited effectiveness, of disability rights like employment equity and the duty to accommodate.

Who Is in the Labour Force?

In 2006, according to Statistics Canada's survey of disability and the Canadian labour force, there were approximately 2.5 million working-age people with disabilities between the ages of fifteen and sixty-four. Just over half of them (51.3 percent) were employed, about 44 percent were not in the labour force, and only 119,340, or 4.9 percent, were unemployed. [14] People are not in the labour force for a variety of reasons, including retirement, school, family responsibilities, discouragement or inability to get a job, or limitations related to the amount or type of work they can do. Those not in the labour force are different from those who are unemployed. Unemployed people are actively seeking employment and able to work.

Chart 2: People with disabilities are much more likely not to even be in the labour force than people without disabilities.

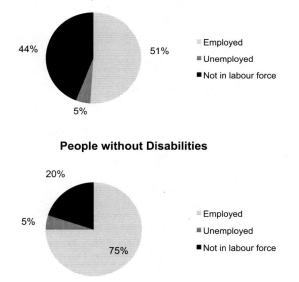

Source: Statistics Canada. 2008. *Participation and Activity Limitation Survey 2006: Labour Force Experience of People with Disabilities in Canada.* Ottawa: Ministry of Industry.

The significance of the situation of people with disabilities in Canada makes greater sense when it is compared with the situation for the same age group of people who do not live with disabilities. Among those people, 75 percent were in the labour force, 20 percent were not in the labour force, and 5 percent were unemployed (see Chart 2).

These differences between the number of people with disabilities who are not in the labour force and those without disabilities are similar in other Western industrialized countries such as the United Kingdom, Australia and the United States.[15] Younger people with

Chart 3: People with disabilities are more likely to not participate in the labour force than people without disabilities. Depending on the age range, the difference can be as high as 30 percent less participation.

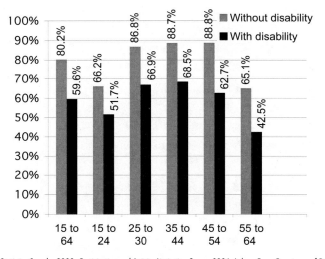

Source: Statistics Canada. 2008. *Participation and Activity Limitation Survey 2006: Labour Force Experience of People with Disabilities in Canada.* Ottawa: Ministry of Industry.

disabilities are most likely to be in the labour force, although the rate at which they participate is still far below the rate of people of the same age without disabilities (See Chart 3).

People with disabilities are also more likely to be unemployed than people without disabilities. The percentage of unemployed people in Chart 2 is different from the unemployment rate. The unemployment rate includes people who are actively searching for work and able to work, and thus measures labour market success of people with disabilities. In 2006, the unemployment rate for working-age people with disabilities was 10.4 percent, while the rate for working-age people without disabilities was 6.8 percent.

The unemployment rate changed depending on where people

lived in Canada, with more people with disabilities unemployed in Quebec and the Atlantic provinces. As well, the Statistics Canada labour force report illustrated differences in the unemployment rates among people with different impairments. Specifically, people with hearing impairments had the lowest unemployment rate among people with disabilities, while people with intellectual disabilities had the lowest labour participation rate.

Statistics Canada's 2006 survey also showed that there were approximately 1.1 million working-age adults with disabilities (43.8 percent) not in the labour force, including people who were retired and less than sixty-five years old. Many people assume that people with disabilities do not work because they are unable to as a result of their impairments. Yet the picture is not that clear. Of those currently working, roughly 40 percent said their condition affected the amount or kind of work they could do. Of those not in the labour force or unemployed, roughly 60 percent reported that they were limited by their impairment or condition in the amount or kind of work they could do. In both cases, it is clear that the ability to work is only partly shaped by the impairments or conditions that people with disabilities live with. Other factors, including discrimination, perceptions of employers and co-workers, a lack of workplace accommodations and systemic barriers such as a lack of accessible transportation, also shape their ability to participate in the labour force.

For those people with disabilities who have employment, there remains a significant gap between their average income and that of people without disabilities. According to Statistics Canada, in 2006, the average employment income for working-age adults with disabilities, $29,393, was 22.5 percent lower than for working-age adults without disabilities, who earn on average $37,994. Those with intellectual disabilities had the lowest average employment income ($18,172), followed by those with mental health disabilities ($19,063) and those with communication disabilities ($19,485). People with hearing disabilities earned the highest average employment income ($32,676).

What do People with Disabilities Need to Enter and Remain in the Labour Force?
In many cases, workplace accommodations are essential to the inclusion of people with disabilities. These may range from a modified workday, special chairs or workstations to accessible elevators or ramps. While many people with disabilities who are in the labour force believe their accommodation needs have been met, there have been some significant gaps and decreases between 2001 and 2006. In addition, for those people with disabilities not in the labour force, the lack of workplace accommodation is often a significant barrier to their ability to get a job. Workplace accommodation is a positive duty for employers and part of disability rights in Canada.

Many people with disabilities face discrimination in their search for work. Statistics Canada reported that in 2006, 25.5 percent of unemployed people with disabilities believed that in the previous five years they had been denied a job because of disability. In a project that monitors and promotes disability rights in Canada and across the world, participants frequently spoke of the discrimination they faced, including in their search for work. For some, the training programs that they wanted to take were not accessible; for others, there were negative assumptions made about their capacity to do a particular job based on disability. One disabled woman living in Toronto said:

> When I've applied for director positions I'm not getting interviews and I'm not sure why…. I suspect that there may be some things, that there's some perceptions about whether I have the stamina or whether I'm energetic enough or whatever.[16]

This discrimination comes despite the human rights legislation and protections at both the federal and provincial levels. As we discuss further in the next section, addressing discrimination in human rights in Canada requires individuals to make complaints.

One significant barrier or disincentive to work for many people with disabilities who are not in the labour force is the loss of benefits if they become employed. For many people with disabilities on provincial social assistance programs, prescription drugs are part of the assistance. If a person with disabilities enters the labour force, they lose this coverage and add some considerable expenses to their life. A disabled woman in Winnipeg put it clearly:

> You may have to be a person who is on social assistance for instance to have any drugs covered at all, whereas if you're a working disabled person and we know this, you are the working poor. How are you going to afford your medications and all the things you need?[17]

A 2010 federal report on disability illustrated the importance of these disincentives to work for people with disabilities: "Approximately 17.6 percent of people who are not in the labour force are discouraged from looking for work because of the potential of losing some or all of their current social transfer income if they work, while 11.5 percent are worried about losing access to their drug plans or housing subsidies."[18] To address these barriers requires a broad approach to providing disability supports, across federal and provincial governments, and coordinating employment-related and income programs for people with disabilities.

Some barriers, including accessible transportation, are outside of individual or employer control and are part of the systemic barriers people with disabilities face on a daily basis that discourage them from looking for work. Ensuring an accessible environment, including accessible transportation, is critical to enabling people with disabilities to enter the labour force.

Employment offers more than income; it also offers a sense of belonging, contributing and being valued. Many people with disabilities who are out of the labour force feel alienated and excluded from their communities. The Independent Living Centre in Newfoundland and Labrador asked people who were not working why they wanted to work. The responses included they would have a place to have an identity, be part of a community, have learning opportunities and better opportunities generally.[19] Employment provides income as well as inclusion in communities and a sense of contributing in a way that is valued in Canadian society.

What Are the Implications of the Labour Market Participation Gap?

More than a million people with disabilities are not in the labour force. Many of them could work with appropriate workplace accommodations or an accessible environment. Most of these people really want to work and contribute.

Employment is one of the measurements of inclusion in Canadian society. By this measurement more than a million people with disabilities are excluded. This has ramifications that extend well beyond the workplace.

Poverty

Poverty is one of the most daunting and stark stories of living with disability in Canada. In 2006, almost half a million working-age people with disabilities lived below the low-income thresholds, which are often called the poverty line. That means one in five working-age Canadians with disabilities are living in poverty. Working-age people with disabilities are twice as likely as those without disabilities to be poor.[20] The poverty line does not include disability-related costs, including aids for mobility, services or medication. Women with disabilities have higher rates of lower income than men with disabilities or women and men without disabilities. More than twice as many women with disabilities who live in low income are single parents. Poverty is significantly higher among Aboriginal people with disabilities, rising to 38 percent, double the rate for non-Aboriginal people with disabilities (see Chart 4).

Part of the story of why poverty is so persistent among people with disabilities is their low participation in the labour force and the type of jobs they do. The Caledon Institute, a social policy think-tank, argued, based on 2006 Statistics Canada data, that "Canadians with

Gloria Looks Forward to Her Future

I have several chronic conditions that make it impossible for me to work in the fields where I was previously employed. I have high blood pressure, asthma, osteoarthritis in my knees, left shoulder and hands, and I also have diabetes. My former occupations were physically demanding. I worked as a construction worker, and have held several positions in the hospitality industry.

After my oldest daughter was born, I started to have health issues, but went ahead and had two more girls. Once my youngest daughter was born, my health deteriorated even further. So, I decided to stay at home and raise my girls.

A couple of years ago, I was diagnosed with diabetes and hit a wall of depression. I had almost given up on life completely. I went from being an outgoing, fun loving person to sitting in front of the television all day. I became a shut in. Grocery shopping and doctors' appointments were the extent of my outings.

I could see that the rut I had allowed myself to fall into was affecting, not only me, but was having a very negative effect on my daughters as well. I knew I had to pick myself up and try to do something.

I have a fair amount of education and was thinking about trying to get back into university, but financially that isn't possible right now. Yet I knew I didn't want to sit on welfare doing nothing for the rest of my life.

One Sunday afternoon I was reading the newspaper and I saw an article about the Neil Squire Society and how they have helped many people with disabilities return to work. I thought maybe I will have a chance to start living again.

I can't say that coming to Employ-Ability class every day has been easy for me. I'm still struggling with the tail end of a very long depression. I know I still haven't been able to accept that this is my life; I will never be able to get off the daily medications that I take.

However, I now have a glimmer of hope. Although I will not be able to return to the life I once knew, I will be able to contribute to society and make a better life for my daughters and for myself. I am looking forward to the future, to getting a job, and being able to support my family.

Source: Neil Squire Society, "Gloria Looks forward to her future" <http://www.neilsquire.ca/success-stories/gloria-future/>. Used with permission.

severe/very severe disabilities have, at most, a tenuous or episodic attachment to the paid labour force. Those who work typically earn low or modest wages in unemployment-prone jobs, and so may have nowhere else to turn but welfare for support."[21]

As noted earlier, employment income is lower for people with disabilities, even when they have the same education as people without disabilities. Employment income is lower among people with severe impairments, and women with disabilities earn considerably less than men with disabilities, and women and men without disabilities.

Working-age people with disabilities outside the labour force rely for income on government programs like Canada/Quebec Pension Plan (C/QPP) Disability, Employment Insurance (EI) Sickness Benefits, private disability benefits plans, workers' compensation and social assistance. Some of these programs, such as EI and social assistance,

Chart 4: Disabled people, particularly disabled Aboriginal people, are as much as twice as likely to be poor than their non-disabled counterparts. Only disabled visible minority persons have poverty rates similar to non-disabled visible minority persons.

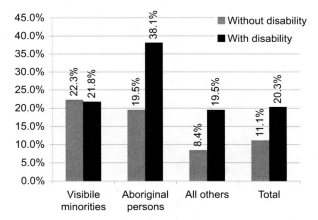

Source: Crawford, Cameron. 2010. *Disabling Poverty and Enabling Citizenship: Understanding the Poverty and Exclusion of Canadians with Disabilities.* <http://ccdonline.ca/en/socialpolicy/poverty-citizenship/demographic-profile/understanding-poverty-exclusion>.

Chart 5: Social assistance rates for people with disabilities are substantially lower than income from full-time minimum wage jobs in all provinces.

Province	Social assistance for person with disability (2010)	Minimum wage rate/ hour (as of Sept. 2011)	Minimum wage at 37 hours/week, 52 weeks/year
Newfoundland and Labrador	$11,182	$10.00	$19,240
Prince Edward Island	$9,350	$9.30	$17,893
Nova Scotia	$9,474	$9.65	$18,567
New Brunswick	$8,670	$9.50	$18,278
Quebec	$10,936	$9.65	$18,567
Ontario	$13,350	$10.25	$19,721
Manitoba	$9,517	$9.50	$18,278
Saskatchewan	$11,195	$9.50	$18,278
Alberta	$9,445 AISH $14,614	$9.40	$18,086
British Columbia	$11,438	$8.75	$16,835

Source: National Council of Welfare, Interactive Welfare Incomes Map, 2010, <http://www.ncw.gc.ca/h.4m.2@-eng.jsp?lang=eng>; Labour Canada, Current and Forthcoming Minimum Hourly Wage Rates for Experienced Adult Workers in Canada <http://srv116.services.gc.ca/dimt-wid/sm-mw/rpt1.aspx?lang=eng>.

were created as a safety net to catch people for short periods as they were out of work. All except social assistance require some employment in order to be eligible for benefits.

Many people with disabilities are not in the labour force and cannot access employment-related benefits like C/QPP or EI. As a result, many people with disabilities turn to provincial social assistance or welfare for income. In 2007, one-half of the welfare caseload across Canada was made up of people with disabilities.[22] A much higher percentage of these social assistance recipients were people with complex or multiple impairments, or those labelled by Statistics Canada as having severe or very severe disabilities.

Social assistance benefits for people with disabilities are the largest source of income for people with disabilities, and provincial governments spent $8.1billion on these benefits in 2008–09.[23] As Chart 5 illustrates, all of these programs provide substantially lower benefits than income from a minimum wage job.

Lack of employment income and a reliance on social assistance benefits lead to poverty for many people with disabilities in Canada.

Disability-Related Costs and Supports

The costs of living with impairments intensify the effects of the labour market gap for people with disabilities and add to the probability of living in poverty for many people. In 2006, nearly two-thirds of the adult population of Canadians with disabilities (2.7 million) said they needed technical aids or specialized equipment to undertake their daily activities.[24] These ranged from hearing aids, magnifiers, computers, canes, reach extenders, hot or cold aids, inhalers and puffers. Sixty percent of these said they had all of their needs met, while the other 40 percent said they had some or none of their needs met. Most people paid for their own assistive devices, and these costs ranged from a few dollars to tens of thousands of dollars. When needs for these disability supports were not met, the costs were the primary reason. The statistics for children with disabilities between the ages of five and fourteen suggest more than half of children with disabilities require aids, although less than half of those had all their needs met. As with adults, parents and families primarily paid the costs of these aids and devices (60.7 percent).

Disability supports also include personal assistance, including help with preparing meals, doing housework, managing personal finances, getting to appointments and doing errands. In 2006, 2.4 million people with disabilities over age fifteen needed help with at least one activity of daily living.[25] Over 80 percent relied on their immediate family to provide this care. However, as their needs for support became more complex and they needed more help, people with disabilities increasingly turned to extended family, friends, neighbours and paid care workers. Paid care workers primarily provided personal care assistance and nursing care.

One of the significant benefits of social assistance for many people with disabilities is the provision of disability supports as part of the welfare package. Usually this includes prescription drug coverage, dental and vision care, and supplementary health benefits. This cuts many of the disability-related costs for those on social assistance, but as the Caledon Institute argues, it means they bump against the "welfare wall":

> Welfare links them to crucial disability supports, but if they manage to move from welfare to the workforce, they may lose access to these vital supports which they often cannot find and afford on their own outside welfare. So once on welfare, many recipients with serious disabilities find it difficult, if not impossible, to leave because that is the only way they can obtain the essential supports they require.[26]

The gap in labour market participation for people with disabilities in addition to low employment income and high disability-related costs have a cascading effect on the lives of people with disabilities, leaving many living in poverty and reliant on provincial social assistance programs and their families for supports.

Disability Rights and Employment Equity

Since the mid-1980s, Canadian law has increasingly recognized the barriers to employment faced by people with disabilities and created tools to assist in removing these barriers. Employment equity and the duty to accommodate are seen as ways to ensure the Canadian labour force is more inclusive of people with disabilities.

The *Employment Equity Act* has two goals for the four groups it covers (women, Aboriginal people, people with disabilities and members of visible minorities): to achieve equality in the workplace and to correct conditions that lead to disadvantage for members of these groups. Employers accountable under this legislation, including the federal public service, federally regulated private companies in areas like banking and transportation, crown corporations and federal contractors,[27] must report on their employment of people in these groups, review and identify any barriers to employment and develop a plan on how they will remove the barriers. To be eligible, people with disabilities are defined as having "a long term or recurring physical, mental, sensory, psychiatric or learning impairment and: considers himself/herself to be disadvantaged in employment by reason of that impairment; or believes that an employer or potential employer is likely to consider him/her to be disadvantaged in employment by reason of that impairment."[28]

Some have argued that employment equity is "reverse discrimination," or an attempt to exclude certain groups by focusing on the inclusion of other groups. Employment equity in Canada has been established to identify those who have been excluded in the past and works to include them. Employment equity does not exclude individuals or groups.

In the sectors that are regulated by employment equity, the rates of labour market participation of persons with disabilities have improved over the past twenty years. In 1987, 1.6 percent of workers in both the federally regulated private sector and the federal public service were persons with disabilities. Twenty years later, in 2007, the federal public service has 5.9 percent of its workforce made up of people with disabilities. The federally regulated private sector has only 2.7 percent representation.[29]

The goal of employment equity is to identify the individual who may be disadvantaged and provide them with a remedy, by targeted hiring, to address their disadvantage. The focus is on the differences among peoples' bodies, not on the environments that may create differences. Many workers believe the environments they work in disable them because the environments do not accommodate their needs and also create them as the exception or the "abnormal" person.

In research for his doctoral dissertation, Jean-Louis Deveau talked with federal public service workers about their experiences as workers with disabilities:

> Kelly's hearing impairment made it impossible for her to make out what people were saying to her on the phone outside the confines of a soundproof workstation; Roberta's epileptic fits, which were triggered by uncontrolled use of personal care products [by others in her workplace], infringed on her autonomy to get to and from her office; and Sahil's hearing impairment made it impossible for him to participate in staff meetings whenever microphones and speakers were omitted because of the background noise caused by a noisy HVAC system…. Kelly's inability to converse with people on the phone was not attributed to the "fact" that there was no soundproof workstation available but to the "fact" that she was a person who had a "long-term or recurring physical, mental, sensory, psychiatric or learning impairment."… This is how we create disability in the Canadian federal public service. People are not hired as disabled workers; they are created as such.[30]

In the workplace, accommodating difference, and especially the formal process of workplace accommodation, becomes the proving ground for the success or failure of employment equity for people with disabilities. Accommodation is both a right and a duty. The right is in the *Canadian Human Rights Act* as well as the *Employment Equity Act* and applies to employers, unions and all employees.[31] It is a broad duty, applied to all workers, including temporary and probationary workers, as well as to all stages of hiring and employment. It requires employers to demonstrate that they have taken every reasonable step, short of undue hardship, to accommodate a worker with disabilities. When workers feel they have not been accommodated, their recourse is to lay a complaint through the Canadian Human Rights Commission, which can be a lengthy and demanding process.

Between 2001 and 2006, there was a significant decline in workplace accommodations. Statistics Canada distinguishes between two types of accommodations: those that are physical or structural (e.g., handrails, modified workstations, accessible washrooms) and those that are resource-specific (e.g., job redesign, a modified work schedule, computer aids). The 2009 Federal Report on Disability states: "In 2006, 70.2% of employed working-age adults with disabilities with requirements had all of their resource-specific workplace modification needs met, compared to 79.9% in 2001. In contrast, 49.1% of those with physical/structural modification requirements indicated that all of their needs were met in 2006, a decrease from 76.1% in 2001."

This suggests that workers with disabilities, even those hired as a result of employment equity, are adapting themselves in order to hold those jobs, rather than being accommodated.

Access to employment brings with it not only increased independence as a result of income but also a sense of belonging and contributing to society. While it appears that more people with disabilities are participating in the labour force, substantial numbers of them are not having their needs for workplace accommodation met. This is not sustainable for workers with disabilities or an indication that they are being included. Indeed, this suggests that employment equity is not working well for people with disabilities, largely because it does not appear to be addressing the systemic gaps that lead to the exclusion of people with disabilities. Without greater progress on transforming workplaces to include the range of diverse human bodies, it is likely that more and more people with disabilities will be forced to leave the workforce and meet with greater poverty.

Transportation

Without accessible public transportation, many people with disabilities cannot go to work or school, get groceries, take their children to the park, do volunteer work, get to health care appointments or visit friends. In other words, accessible public transportation is a critical element of building an inclusive society.

A 2010 study by Transport Canada reports that approximately 2.8 million Canadians with disabilities undertake at least one "long-distance" (over 80 km) trip per year. Of these, 1.3 million have "mobility needs requiring assistance whose travel could be jeopardized by inaccessibility features of the transportation system."[32] The study reports that 800,000 are able to use the transportation system with difficulty. An additional 700,000 people with disabilities are currently prevented from long-distance travel because of the inaccessibility of the transportation system. The authors report that 25–30 percent of people with disabilities do not get their accessibility needs met within the existing transportation system.

In Canada, federal and provincial governments share responsibility for transportation. Through the Canadian Transportation Agency (CTA), the federal government is responsible for air, rail, interprovincial buses and marine ferries. The *Canadian Transportation Act* specifically identifies responsibility for accessible transportation for people with disabilities. The CTA responds to individual complaints and develops regulations and codes of practice and standards for accessibility.

The provincial and municipal governments are responsible for urban and rural public transportation. Provincial human rights commissions can provide some recourse for complaints about accessible transportation, since there is a duty to accommodate those who are disadvantaged in public services including public transportation. In 2011 in Ontario, the *Accessibility for Ontarians with Disabilities Act* (2005) resulted in the introduction of the Integrated Accessibility Standards, which relate to public transportation.

Urban Public Transportation

Accessible public transportation means several different things. It can mean the creation of parallel transportation systems for people with disabilities. Most urban areas have systems that usually provide door-to-door service available to registered users who pre-book. With an increase in the aging population, these services are being more and more strained, and there are no common standards in terms of costs, eligibility or access. Accessible public transportation is often very limited for people with disabilities in rural and remote communities.

Increasingly, urban transportation systems are integrating accessibility in their mainstream services through the use of low-floor buses, accessible stations and terminals, tactile way-finding and greater use of online and audio trip planning tools. While access is improving for many people, getting accommodation takes complaints from users before action is taken. For example, David Lepofsky, a blind transit user and lawyer, had been working since 1995 to get the Toronto Transit Commission (TTC) to call out the stops on buses and streetcars. He made a complaint in 2005 to the Ontario Human Rights Commission, which was settled in 2007.[33] Accessible public transportation has not been recognized as an essential public service and may be lost in the funding battles between municipal and provincial governments.

Air and Rail Travel

Accessible transportation has been an issue for the disability advocacy movement since its beginnings in the 1970s. The CCD has taken its concerns to the CTA through its advisory committee as well as by formal complaints. In the late 2000s, after extremely lengthy and expensive legal battles, two major victories removed some obstacles for travel for people with disabilities.

In 2008, the CTA, with a follow-up decision by the Supreme Court of Canada, decided that airlines could not charge a second fare to people with disabilities who required a second seat for their

Claire Mehta

At age 52, Claire Mehta knows all about uphill battles. Under her maiden name, Clariss Kelly, she was the original complainant in what became a lengthy battle with VIA Rail over passenger cars that are inaccessible to wheelchairs.

The case went right up to the Supreme Court of Canada, which ruled only last year that, under the Canadian Charter of Rights and Freedoms, people with disabilities have a right to barrier-free transportation.

"The VIA decision shows that the standards we uphold should be based not on costs but on human rights issues," says Pat Danforth, chair of the transportation committee of the Council of Canadians with Disabilities.

In Europe and the U.S., "they look at cases like VIA as state of the art," says David Baker, a lawyer who has been a central player in some of the most significant disability rights cases, including VIA. "But in terms of actual access, we're still the pits," he adds.

"There's more of an awareness that disabled people should be part of everything today," says Mehta. "But there's still a long way to go." Battling to be recognized costs a lot, emotionally and financially, she says. "It takes a lot to continue."

Today, asked about her future plans, she says "I want to take a nice, long train trip across Canada."

Source: Helen Henderson. "Special Means to an End," *Toronto Star*, March 18, 2008. <thestar.com/living/Disabilities/article/347009>. Used with permission.

attendant or as a result of their impairment. The CCD had made this complaint in 2002, although the issue had been an advocacy focus since the 1980s, when the *Obstacles* report recommended "one person one fare."[34]

One year earlier, the CCD won a significant Supreme Court of Canada victory requiring VIA Rail to change rail cars it had bought that did not provide access to many people with disabilities. Using disability rights, the Supreme Court of Canada argued that VIA Rail had an obligation to accommodate people with disabilities and had not demonstrated that making the rail cars accessible would cause undue hardship.[35]

The CCD identifies the following ongoing access issues for people with disabilities:

- Greater use of small planes that cannot carry a standard wheelchair in the cargo hold.
- Small plane use means less access to boarding ramps and deplaning onto the tarmac.
- Inadequate space for guide dogs in flight.
- Even after winning a 7-year legal battle with VIA Rail over their purchase of inaccessible passenger cars a member of CCD could not travel by train from Toronto to Vancouver for the Paralympics…
- Introduction of body scanners without any study or determination if they will be accessible. If not accessible, people with disabilities will be required to submit to the more intrusive "pat down."
- Installation by airlines of inaccessible entertainment systems. The system was accessible to persons with vision impairments before but the new system is not.
- Although ordered to do so interprovincial bus systems that span neighbouring communities refuse to call out bus stops.[36]

Accessible public transportation in all of its forms requires both universally designed systems that allow flexibility and accessibility for the greatest number of people and specific accommodations for those whose needs are outside of what can be accommodated through universal design. As a public service, standards should be determined by the relevant government in close consultation with users with disabilities, rather than in response to individual complaints and lengthy legal cases, which is how the existing system works.

Telecommunications

An increasingly important part of everyday life is access to telecommunications and information technologies. These technologies include not only computers with access to the Internet, but also wireless and cell phones, "smart" phones, tablet computers, relevant apps, GPS units, music players like MP3 players and touch screen service kiosks like ticket dispensers. People with disabilities use these technologies, although more young people with disabilities use them than older people with disabilities. In 2005–06, roughly half of adults with disabilities used the Internet.[37] People with disabilities are also significant users of cell phones and ATM banking machines.[38]

Information technologies have the potential to remove many barriers for people with disabilities. People with vision impairments and learning disabilities use computers to read print to them. Many deaf people use smart phones to text others, eliminating the use of sign interpreters at times. People with intellectual disabilities are using video sharing websites as a way of telling their stories and gathering information. Closed captioning on televisions helps many people, including those who are hard of hearing, to understand what is being said. Descriptive video makes movies accessible to blind moviegoers by describing the visual scenes in words. Email, Facebook and Twitter all provide many ways to connect with peers for support, friendship and other relationships and can help to reduce isolation.

Disability Rights, Telecommunications and Broadcasting

Given the possibilities for inclusion as a result of information technologies and telecommunications, as well as the incredibly fast pace of change in this area, access for people with disabilities is essential. The Canadian Radio-television Telecommunications Commission (CRTC) monitors and regulates telecommunications and broadcasting in Canada under the *Telecommunications Act*. Part of its mandate is to regulate accessibility. Until 2008, much of its work on accessibility was in response to individual complaints.

In 2008, the CRTC held public hearings on issues related to accessibility in telecommunications and broadcasting. Many people with disabilities told the hearing about the barriers as a result of inaccessible cell phones, telephone equipment, websites and limited closed captioning, to mention a few. In 2009, the CRTC adopted a new policy — *Broadcasting and Telecom Regulatory Policy 2009–430* — on accessibility in telecommunications and broadcasting services.

Several key disability organizations, including the Canadian Association of the Deaf and ARCH Disability Law Centre, have led the advocacy work, including making complaints to the CRTC. In particular, ARCH has argued that inaccessibility is the same as discrimination and the CRTC should therefore regulate telecommunications in a manner consistent with equality and anti-discrimination requirements in the Canadian Charter of Rights and Freedoms and

---

Donna Jodhan

Donna Jodhan was one of the first blind people in Canada to earn an MBA, in 1981, and one of the first in the world to obtain technical certifications from software companies Microsoft and Novell.

So the Toronto accessibility consultant was shocked in 2004 when she had trouble applying for a position posted on the federal government's jobs website.

Despite her considerable technical expertise — she has won four accessibility design awards from IBM — Jodhan couldn't get Ottawa's online job application to work, even after repeated calls to the government helpline.

When Ottawa offered residents the option of filling out the 2006 Census online, Jodhan was thwarted once again.

"The Internet is something that is liberating to everybody — but not to blind and visually impaired Canadians," she said in an interview. "Canada used to be at the top when it came to accessibility 10 years ago. It's way down the list now."

On Tuesday [September 21, 2010], Jodhan will argue in federal court that her inability to apply for a position on the federal jobs website or complete the online version of the 2006 Census breached her equality rights under the Canadian Charter of Rights and Freedoms.

She will also argue that this violation and her ongoing inability to access the government's online information and services constitute a breach against all blind and partially sighted Canadians, said Jodhan's lawyer David Baker.

About 3 million Canadians have visual or other impairments that make it difficult to access the Internet.

"It is just so frustrating that (the visually impaired) can't access government information, can't apply for government jobs — can't use the Internet. That's what this case is about," Baker said in an interview.

Blind people visit websites using screen reader software which converts text to speech. But the software can't work unless a web page includes special coding, Baker said.

American and European governments have adopted the latest international web accessibility standards for their websites as have Canadian banks and many businesses, he said. But the Canadian government has not — even though the changes would not be difficult or expensive to implement, he said.

Jodhan, who launched her case in 2006 under the now defunct Court Challenges program which helped fund equality rights cases, wants the court to order Ottawa to upgrade its websites to the latest accessibility standards within 12 months and monitor compliance.

In its written defence, the federal government argues that the Charter's goal of providing "substantive equality" and "reasonable accommodation" to Jodhan were met through telephone help lines, by mail and in person.

Internet access to government services and information is not a right guaranteed in law, the government says in its written submission to the court. "Alternative channels available did allow (Jodhan) to access services and information independently, in a manner that respected her privacy and dignity," it says.

With more than 120 government departments and agencies and more than 23 million web pages, "it is unlikely that the government's web presence will ever be perfectly accessible to all," it adds.

A spokesperson for the federal government said Ottawa is working to make its online information as accessible as possible.

Ontario lawyer and disability rights activist David Lepofsky is waging a battle to make the provincial government's websites and services accessible.

Lepofsky, who is blind, is particularly upset that the province's new Presto electronic transit card is not accessible to the visually impaired and others.

Ontario is offering to adopt the most current international web accessibility standards, but Queen's Park is giving itself up to 2018 and even longer for other organizations to get started, he noted.

"This is ridiculous," Lepofsky said in an interview. "When it comes to creating new technology, experts have shown that there is… no significant added burden on organizations to adopt the latest standards for full accessibility. Moreover, accessibility for us usually helps lots of people, including those with no disability.

"There is absolutely no reason why any government in this country isn't now complying with the latest international standards," he added.

Update: On November 29, 2010, Justice Michael Kelen of the Federal Court ruled in favour of Donna Jodhan that the federal government must ensure its websites are accessible to visually-impaired Canadians. The federal government has appealed that decision.

Source: Laurie Monsebraaten. 2010. "Blind Woman Says Federal Websites Discriminate against the Visually Impaired." *thestar.com* September 19. <http://www.thestar.com/news/gta/article/863379-blind-woman-says-federal-websites-discriminate-against-the-visually-impaired>. Used with permission.

the *Canadian Human Rights Act*. This argument recognizes that, in the context of a knowledge-based society, where access to telecommunications can be critical to inclusion more generally in society, inaccessible telecommunications is a significant barrier.

In 2009, the CRTC recognized the need for its policies to be consistent with the Charter and stated: "In considering whether or not the proposed accommodations are reasonable, the Commission has also utilized leading Canadian human rights principles that recognize that equality is a fundamental value and central component of the public interest."

Accessible Equipment

In 2001, Chris and Marie Stark of Ottawa asked the CRTC to overturn its 1994 decision to stop regulating wired phone equipment, arguing that phones had become more complex and inaccessible since that decision. Finally, in 2007, after years of submissions, including objections from most of Canada's major telephone companies, the CRTC denied the Starks' request and refused to re-regulate phone equipment. The CRTC argued that it encourages telecommunications service providers to provide consumers with information about equipment with accessibility features. The 2009 CRTC policy requires wireless phone providers to provide at least one model that is accessible for "the needs of people who are blind and/or have moderate-to-severe mobility or cognitive disabilities."

In 2011, Bell Canada asked the CRTC to use part of a fund that had been protected for increased access for people with disabilities, called the deferral accounts fund,[39] to develop more accessible mobile equipment.[40] Given Bell's prominence in the market, the indication that it will use the principles of universal/inclusive design and will draw upon the expertise from an advisory group of representatives of people with disabilities, may stimulate further development in this area.

Inaccessible equipment continues to be a barrier to information technologies for people with disabilities. Equipment that is fully accessible can often be very expensive since it is targeted to a small audience, which puts such devices out of reach of many people with disabilities. Using the principles of universal or inclusive design in the development of new equipment, including having multiple ways of operating a device, ensures a wider audience for devices.

Broadcasting

While there has been increasing access for television users through closed captioning and some limited described video, the CRTC's 2009 policy includes some significant increases. Closed captioning is to be available for all of the broadcast day, and described video for all channels is to be available for four hours per week. These are improvements but do not yet meet the advocacy group Access 2020's goal of 100 percent access for all users by 2020.

The CRTC also ruled in 2011, in its decision on the acquisition of CTV by BCE, that an independent broadcast accessibility fund of $5.7 million must be created and required that the directors of this fund be "persons with disabilities, representatives of disability organizations and/or other parties with relevant expertise in developing or implementing accessibility solutions."[41] One area not regulated by any of the recent developments is the downloading of television programs on the Internet.

As new technologies emerge quickly, accessibility often gets lost. Telecommunications companies that develop and market devices do not have a good record of voluntarily creating accessible equipment or services. Recent decisions by the CRTC related to accessibility create greater expectations for the provisions of some accessibility for telecommunications and broadcasting. Other countries, including the United States, have legislation that requires telecommunications equipment manufacturers and service providers to ensure accessibility for people with disabilities. In Canada, the measure of the success of these decisions and identifying the gaps in accessibility will be up to users of these technologies, including users with disabilities.

Health Care

As with most Canadians, people with disabilities rely on Canada's public health care system to identify and address health care concerns and promote well-being. Ensuring access to health care and removing barriers for people with disabilities is an important part of disability rights in Canada. But health care is complicated for people with disabilities because of widespread assumptions, often called the medical model of disability, which equate disability with illness or conditions — those "problems" that we expect health care providers to remedy. When disability is reduced to a health issue or concern, it is seen as something to be "fixed," primarily by health care providers, rather than as a set of barriers and assumptions that need to be addressed within society as a whole. Indeed, many health care providers only regard disability as a physical or mental deficit. Many disability policies and programs reinforce that view when they require physicians to provide administrative documentation about a person's condition and confirm their eligibility for social or income programs on the basis of their deficiencies, such as not being able to work a full day or walk a certain distance unassisted.

As well, it is in the health care system where people with disabilities experience significant paternalism — "all for their own good," of course. These attempts to make decisions on behalf of people with disabilities, using the care provider's understanding of "what is best" for the person with disabilities, undermine the independence and autonomy of people with disabilities and the right to make choices about their own lives and health care.

Disability Rights and Health Care

When the *Canada Health Act*, the legislation that provides the framework for the universal health care system in Canada, talks about accessibility it does not specifically include accessibility for people with disabilities. In 1997, the Supreme Court of Canada, however, ruled on access to sign language interpreters in a British Columbia hospital. The Eldridge decision was a significant inclusion of disability rights in health care and government services more generally. The Court ruled that the failure to provide sign language interpretation for deaf people was discrimination and meant that deaf people did not benefit equally from health care services.

In addition to that understanding of disability rights, the UN-CRPD, which Canada has ratified and agreed to implement, recognizes the rights of disabled people to health care, to rehabilitation, to live in the community rather than institutions and to have a say in their own treatment. Together these provide an important basis for addressing the existing barriers to health care for people with disabilities in Canada that result from the attitudes and assumptions of health care providers about disability and the accessibility of health care environments and policies.

Health Care Needs and Usage

Despite the fact that many people with disabilities are high users of health care services, there remains a significant amount of unmet needs for health care among people with disabilities. MaryAnn McColl, a professor and health policy analyst, suggests that working-age adults with disabilities in Canada are three times more likely to have unmet health needs than non-disabled Canadians.[42] In 2006, 15 percent of adults with disabilities were not able to get the health care services they needed, and it was higher for those with complex impairments and conditions.[43]

Even though Canada has a legislated universal not-for-profit health care system, which is meant to ensure that lack of income does not create barriers to health care, for people with disabilities the greatest deterrent to receiving the care they need is, in fact, cost. Disabled people have three different reasons for seeing health professionals: health-related issues experienced by the general population, disability-specific issues and administrative issues related to disability pensions, benefits and services. The latter two sets of issues increase the usage of health care services, and the administrative issues often have associated costs. As well, the costs may result from a visit that is not covered by insurance.

The 2010 Federal Disability Report states that roughly one-quarter of Canadians with disabilities had out-of-pocket costs associated with visiting a health professional in 2005–06, with an average cost of $642.58.[44] Interestingly, more young disabled people had costs than seniors with disabilities. These are often hidden costs, such as fees for completing eligibility forms for benefits, which along with low income or unemployment, may create barriers to health care for people with disabilities.

In addition, many people with disabilities had significant unmet needs in terms of medication and disability-related aids. Again, cost was the most significant barrier to getting these needs met. Thirteen percent of adults with disabilities were unable to get their medication needs met because of costs, with younger working-age adults most likely to have unmet needs.

Costs related to medication, disability aids and uninsured visits to health professionals are some of the extra costs associated with disability in Canada. These are often hidden but significant barriers to accessing health care and ensuring ongoing health. But the barriers for people with disabilities are also a result of inaccessible physical environments and the attitudes and knowledge of health care providers, as well as the system of delivering care.

Access to Health Care

Four types of barriers shape the access people with disabilities have to health care in Canada: physical, attitudinal, expertise and systemic. While much of the lack of access for people with disabilities has been identified in primary health care, similar barriers have been recognized in cancer care and palliative care.[45]

Physical barriers include office equipment such as nonadjustable examination tables, office arrangements such as doors and hallways that are not wide enough for wheelchairs, and access to the office such as accessible transportation and parking. These barriers can often be addressed by an accessibility audit of medical facilities or the use of universal design when designing health care services.

Attitudinal barriers reflect assumptions and stereotypes about disability and people with disabilities that are held by care providers, the conflation of disability with illness and the tendency to over or under attribute other health problems to impairment in diagnosis and treatment. Many of these barriers are the result of broader societally held attitudes that care providers may not realize they hold. To address these requires some recognition of what these negative attitudes may be and how they might affect care. Psychiatrist and palliative care researcher Harvey Chochinov asks: "Might an assumption of poor quality of life in a patient with longstanding disabilities lead to the withholding of life sustaining choices?"[46] As ways to uncover and address these attitudes, Chochinov suggests critical self-reflection in the context of each patient, including asking questions about assumptions as part of case reviews and clinical teaching, undertaking ongoing professional development that challenges and questions providers' attitudes and assumptions and creating a culture within the health care setting where these issues are raised, addressed and become part of the standard of care.

Regardless of the critical reflection about attitudes, many health care providers also do not have knowledge or expertise about impairments, conditions and disability and their interaction with more standard health care issues. This gap affects access to health care for many people with disabilities. People with disabilities often have difficulty finding a primary health care provider with the necessary expertise and availability. For some, this means using specialist services to address primary care needs, which is not always a good use of resources. In all cases, the amount of time required to educate the health care provider about the person's specific circumstances is significant and often requires longer appointments.

Part of this education could take place much earlier, including in medical school. For over twenty years, a group of community activists and professors delivered a module for medical school students in Winnipeg and included people with disabilities as teachers for this unit. Their evaluation of what they found in particular about end-of-life and people with disabilities illustrates both the attitudes and the actions that are possible with this approach. One student commented:

> It's important to hear… the side of the story from people who are actually living with those conditions and how they feel… presented in a light of : I'm being open about my feelings… I want to learn from these people so that (I) don't make these mistakes, so that (I) can be the best doctor (I) can be.[47]

This education needs to be broadly focused, including information about specific conditions, practical issues about medical procedures and discussions of the human rights of people with disabilities.[48] When health care is approached as a partnership between providers and recipients, there is more likely to be better quality of care as well as greater respect for those receiving care.

But there remain some systemic barriers resulting from the model of delivering health care in Canada. Health and disability researcher MaryAnn McColl and her associates suggest that there is greater accessibility and willingness to make accommodations for people with disabilities (such as longer appointments, home-based visits, more accessible premises, etc.) in medical practices in which physicians are paid salaries rather than fees for services.[49] Salaried practices are more often found in urban settings, are large and include multiple disciplines. These factors also mean that there can be better coordination between different service providers, including physicians, home care providers, rehabilitation services and social workers.

What Does This Mean for People with Disabilities?

It is easy to get overwhelmed when reading about the barriers that people with disabilities live with, the gaps between disability rights and the lack of inclusion and access in education, employment, transportation, telecommunications and health care. But these aren't abstract barriers or meaningless statistics. They are the summary of barriers real people face every day. In the next chapter, we examine several solutions that address barriers related to disability and include people with disabilities as integral part of Canadian society.

4. HOW CAN PEOPLE WITH DISABILITIES CLAIM THEIR RIGHTS?

There is a gap between the actual lives of most Canadians with disabilities and the disability rights that are legislated in Canada and articulated in the United Nations Convention of the Rights of Persons with Disabilities (UNCRPD). This chapter explores what is required to ensure that Canadians with disabilities are able to claim their own rights. In some areas, like transportation and health care, exclusion is evident in the lack of access to services that most non-disabled Canadians take for granted. Some people with disabilities are and have been in institutions, long-term care homes and "special education" classrooms that keep them separate and outside of mainstream Canadian society. Many people with disabilities in Canada live in poverty because they are not able to get a job or receive the required disability-related accommodations for work or face discriminatory attitudes about disability. The previous chapters told difficult stories of people subjected to neglect, violence and, sometimes, abuse leading to their deaths. Their stories remind us of the broader societal assumptions about people with disabilities, including that it is better to be dead than disabled and that some disabled people are not worthy of the rights and protections enjoyed by Canadians in general.

Given these accounts of living with disabilities, it is difficult not to be overwhelmed by what is required to ensure that people with disabilities are the subject of human rights. Being a subject rather than an object of human rights means people with disabilities are able to make decisions about their lives and future, they are able to claim rights on their own behalf, and they are able to participate actively in Canadian society. Disability rights activists have proposed new solutions that transform Canadian society to include people with disabilities and enable them to claim disability rights. Moreover, including disabled people and honouring their dignity, autonomy and rights enables all of us to stretch and enhance our understandings of what it means to be human and live in a world of relationships of support and care.

After almost thirty years of disability rights embedded in the Canadian Charter of Rights and Freedoms and the consistent presence of barriers, poverty and exclusion for people with disabilities, many argue that some significant and transformative measures are needed within Canadian society. It is not enough to have stated disability rights, it is essential to be able to claim those rights and reject discrimination. People, however, require capacity and resources to claim their rights. Three concrete solutions to enhance capacity and transform Canadian society are universal or inclusive design, disability supports and income supports. In addition, disability rights advocates call for a more elusive solution — that of belonging and being home.

Universal or Inclusive Design

As the earlier chapters note, Canadians with disabilities face barriers to access in many parts of society as a result of environments — physical, natural and technological — that have been built to accommodate able-bodied people. Electrical lights in a room give access and support to those with sight but are irrelevant to those who are blind. We as a society accept the need for lighting and do

Principles of Universal Design

Equitable Use: The design is useful and marketable to people with diverse abilities. Provides the same means of use for all users: identical whenever possible, equivalent when not; avoids segregating or stigmatizing any user; makes provisions for privacy, security, and safety equally available to all users; makes the design appealing to all users.

Flexibility in Use: The design accommodates a wide range of individual preferences and abilities. Provides choice in methods of use; accommodates left- or right-handed access and use; facilitates the user's accuracy and precision; provides adaptability to the user's pace.

Simple and Intuitive: The use of the design is easy to understand, regardless of the user's experience, knowledge, language skills, or current concentration level. Eliminates unnecessary complexity; is consistent with the user's expectations and intuition; accommodates a wide range of literacy and language skills; arranges information consistent with its importance; provides effective prompting and feedback during and after task completion.

Perceptible Information: The design communicates necessary information effectively to the user, regardless of ambient conditions or the user's sensory abilities. Uses different modes for redundant presentation of essential information; maximizes legibility of essential information; differentiates elements in ways that can be described; provides compatibility with a variety of techniques or devices used by people with sensory limitation.

Tolerance for Errors: The design minimizes hazards and the adverse consequences of accidental or unintended actions. Arranges elements to minimize hazards and errors: The most used elements are the most accessible; hazardous elements are eliminated, isolated or shielded; provides warnings of hazards and errors; provides fail-safe features; discourages unconscious action in tasks that require vigilance.

Low Physical Effort: The design can be used efficiently and comfortably and with a minimum of fatigue; allows the user to maintain a neutral body position; uses reasonable operating forces; minimizes repetitive actions; minimizes sustained physical effort.

Size and Space for Approach and Use: Appropriate size and space is provided for approach, reach, manipulation, and use; provides a clear line of sight to important elements for any seated or standing user; makes the reach to all components comfortable for any seated or standing user;

accommodates variations in hand and grip size; provides adequate space for the use of assistive devices or personal assistance.

not see it as an accommodation. Yet we resist accommodations or universally designed initiatives that would bring the same sense of inclusion for people with disabilities. Sidewalks have been built with curbs that prevent wheelchair users from easy travel. Curb cuts removed that barrier and have the additional benefit of providing greater ease for parents pushing strollers and children riding bicycles or rollerblading. This is an example of universal or inclusive design in practice. Similar electronic "curb cuts" have resulted from applying the principles of universal design to the development of information and communications technologies. Educators are increasingly recognizing the need to apply the principles in order to make it possible for as many learners as possible to have access to curriculum materials and activities.

In 1997, the Center for Universal Design at North Carolina State University developed the widely recognized principles of universal design, and as the principles have gained more recognition, the approach is also called inclusive design. The principles are widely used by architects, engineers, urban planners and many others. Specifically they call for environments that are equitable, flexible, intuitive, perceptible, safe, easy and accommodating.

The use of these principles in the design of buildings and environments has meant greater access and ease of use not only for people with disabilities but for seniors, children, people with low levels of literacy and many others. When they are used in the creation of new public buildings such as hospitals, schools, airports, hotels, museums, band offices, libraries and so on, they increase access for everyone. With increased access and fewer barriers, wheelchair or walker users, people who are blind or hard-of-hearing and people who are unable to comprehend or read complicated instructions have access to places they have not been able to use previously. With that access comes a greater sense of belonging, not being excluded by physical barriers and being able to use the resources available in those buildings.

The same is true in the physical environment. When hiking trails are designed with these principles in mind, more people can use them and be active. When playgrounds are designed inclusively, children with disabilities can join their peers on the structures and not feel like bystanders during recess, for example. When public parks are designed to include, more people can enjoy them.

Creating buildings that are inclusively designed is more difficult when the buildings are old and if they are private homes. Adding universal design features to an existing building requires an audit to identify barriers and retrofitting or changing features that exclude. It can be more costly to retrofit older buildings than to design new buildings using inclusive design. Recent legislation in Ontario, the *Accessibility for Ontarians with Disabilities Act* (AODA), ensures that public spaces are accessible. Building codes, which are under different levels of government, including municipal, provincial and federal, identify the extent to which each building, and under what circumstances, must ensure access for all.

One movement, promoted for example by the Manitoba government, is to ensure that private homes are visitable, which means zero steps into the entryway, level access and wider doors within the home for a visitor and a washroom on the main floor.[1] This approach, which can be used by anyone to modify their home, removes some barriers to visitors and helps people to feel as if they belong and are welcome in another's home.

The principles of universal design have also been adapted to the development and use of information and communications technologies. It is easier for everyone to use new information technologies when they apply universal or inclusive design principles, such as having multiple ways to operate a device. For example, multiple ways to use a cell phone or "smart" phone may include operating it by voice or touch. Some measures to improve access on cell phones, including for those over fifty, who may need reading glasses, include larger screens and buttons. Reading information on a computer screen can be done either visually or through screen reading technology that allows the user to hear it. In many cases, technologies that were developed initially to ensure accessibility for a small group of users have become mainstream. One of the best examples is voice-recognition software that allows users to say what they want to type and have the computer do it for them. It was created for blind users but has been widely used by others who want that additional way to input material in their computers.

As with universal design in buildings, it is easier and cheaper to develop information technologies from the beginning using universal design principles, than either to create special "accessible" technologies for a very small audience or to find "adaptive" solutions to mainstream technologies that have already been developed.

One final area where universal design has become a baseline is in the area of education. In universal educational design, learning materials and methods are created accessible for every student regardless of their ability. This includes having materials available in multiple formats, such as print, electronic and audio. It may include access through screen readers or captioning. It also means flexible materials and activities that provide alternatives for students with differing abilities. Universal design may also support learning by reinforcing information with summaries of key points and important details.

In each of these areas — physical and natural environment, information and communications technologies and learning — the use of universal design in the creation and development ensures access for more people. The use of these inclusive principles means that people with differing ways of using environments, learning and information technologies are included rather than segregated through "special" measures. And as curb cuts illustrate, the features to ensure access can make access easier for many and unexpected groups of people.

Disability Supports

As a result of living in a world created for and geared to non-disabled people, people with disabilities face many barriers that result in poverty and exclusion. One of the first steps to removing barriers is providing disability-related supports. These supports may be aids and devices, personal assistance or environmental accommodations. The Roeher Institute, a research institute associated with the CACL, defined disability supports as "any good, service or environmental adaptation that assists persons with disabilities to overcome limitations in carrying out activities of daily living and in participating in the social, economic, political and cultural life of the community."[2]

The flexibility in this definition is essential given the variation in experiences of barriers among people with disabilities — barriers for some may be inclusive strategies for another. The needs of people with disabilities also change over time, depending on the stage of life they are at as well as the transitions they experience. For example, supports needed when someone is attending school may differ from those required when participating in community volunteer activities. Different supports may be available or needed in different settings. For example, what a child needs at school may not be the same as what they need at home, although there may be some overlap. The supports they need to play sports may be different again. As well, many conditions and impairments change over time. Someone who had polio as a child may have had supports as they grew up but need different supports, including a machine to help with breathing while they sleep, as they experience post polio. Disability supports are also shaped by life transitions, including from childcare to school, from school to work, and from job to job or retirement.

Any comprehensive strategy to address barriers must reflect the complexities of lived experiences with disabilities. As the disability advocacy organizations argue to governments, with disability supports that are flexible and responsive to stage of life and transitions, people with disabilities can learn, contribute to their communities, get paid work and raise families.

People with disabilities in Canada need disability supports in all forms, and many people are doing without because of the costs. In addition, there is a significant reliance on immediate family to provide ongoing support for their family members with disabilities. This unpaid work often goes unrecognized but is clearly critical to the well-being and inclusion of most people with disabilities.

Since 1998, the federal, provincial and territorial governments have recognized the need for policy action related to disability supports. *In Unison* identified disability supports as necessary to ensuring that people with disabilities achieve full citizenship. The report had a vision of improved access, enhanced portability (that is, being able to move from province to province and still receive similar supports), greater responsiveness to individual needs and greater control by the person with disabilities.

In 2004, the federal government commissioned a public opinion poll about Canadian attitudes towards people with disabilities. Most of the respondents saw a significant role for government in addressing barriers to people with disabilities: "By a wide margin, Canadians believe governments have the primary role for supporting people with disabilities when it comes to providing good health care, reliable transportation, specialized equipment, and good education."[3]

The federal, provincial and territorial governments confirmed their commitments to providing a comprehensive system of disability supports in 2005: "The focus for achieving (the full inclusion of Canadians with disabilities) will be joint work with emphasis on improving access to and funding for disability supports and services and for income supports for persons with disabilities, at the same time working to build public awareness and stakeholder and government support to address the challenges facing people with disabilities."[4]

The disability advocacy community reiterated its commitment to new investments in disability-related supports as a priority in the National Action Plan, adopted in 2007 and reaffirmed in its national meetings since then.

While the need for disability supports is great, the costs of a comprehensive program to meet these needs are very high. Governments have been reluctant to implement a program with such significant costs, and, with the responsibility for disability supports at the provincial level, there remains a piecemeal group of programs across the country to provide disability supports.

The disability community has suggested that one way to address the costs of a disability supports program is to recognize the current huge spending of provincial governments on social assistance for people with disabilities. If an income support program was put into place (preferably by the federal government) this would reduce provincial costs and release funds for disability supports programs. While this strategy would shift the costs for income from the provincial social assistance programs to a federal income support program, it would not necessarily increase overall spending.

One question that has not been addressed by either governments or the disability advocacy groups is: How does this approach to disability supports address the needs of Aboriginal people with disabilities? For Aboriginal people who live in urban centres and so have access to provincial services, the impact will be similar to that on non-Aboriginal people with disabilities. But for people with disabilities who live on First Nations communities, one approach to disability supports could include increased federal transfers to First Nations governments targeted for community-based disability supports. In addition, there could be federal/provincial/territorial/Indigenous government cooperation to create clusters of services in remote regions, rather than paying for service recipients to leave their communities and fly to urban centres for services.

For Canadians with disabilities to enjoy their disability rights, not only do they need accessible and inclusive environments, but they also need access to disability supports. The solutions to ensure disability rights are complex and intertwined, involving multiple levels of government, creative thinking about changes to existing programs and ongoing supports provided by family members.

Income Supports

Why is there such persistent and intense poverty among people with disabilities in Canada? As illustrated in Chapter 3, part of the story is about the barriers. People with disabilities, and especially those with complex or severe impairments, have more barriers to education than people without disabilities. Systemic barriers to employment result in a significant gap in labour market participation. High costs are associated with living with disabilities, including costs associated with necessary disability-related supports. Barriers exist to systems of transportation, telecommunications and health care. Each of these sets of barriers, in addition to stigmatizing attitudes about disability, limit the opportunities for full citizenship and participation for people with disabilities and can result in a life with poverty and exclusion. What solutions can transform this poverty trap into something that enhances the rights, dignity and autonomy of people with disabilities?

The disability advocacy community has called for a creative and long-term solution, such as a federal government-led income support program that is similar in structure to the Guaranteed Income Support (GIS) available to low-income seniors. They call for federal-provincial-territorial cooperation to use the savings that come from reducing the number of people with disabilities on social assistance and redirect those savings to the creation of disability supports programs in all provinces and territories. One proposal, described below, suggested an increase in spending by the federal government of $5 billion and a shifting of allocations by the provincial governments from social assistance to disability supports programs of $2.6 billion.

Since 2007, different models have been developed, but the 2010 Caledon Institute proposal for a basic income plan targeted to people labelled with severe disabilities has the greatest momentum and clarity. It is intended to be an income security program, with recipients receiving enough income to pay their rent and buy food and clothes. The proposal argues that a general program for all people with disabilities would not be politically acceptable, since many are able and willing to work with the right supports in place. Rather, the program would be targeted to those who are unable to earn a living from employment as a result of the barriers related to disability. This group includes those labelled as having severe or very severe disabilities.

The plan would provide the same benefits as the GIS as well as funds from a rejigged and refundable disability tax credit. The current disability tax credit is not refundable and is only of benefit to people who have sufficient income to receive a tax refund. A refundable tax credit would be available to all people with disabilities as recognition of the extra costs related to disability and would be available even to people with no taxable income.

The basic income plan, together with a refundable disability tax credit, would begin to provide a stable source of income for people with disabilities who have had to rely on social assistance. But these two, as the Caledon Institute recognizes, need to be accompanied by comprehensive provincial disability supports programs that are not linked to income assistance programs and relatively consistent across the country. To have such a national disability supports program would be a true mark of inclusion and recognition of the ways in which disability shapes all of our lives and is a responsibility of all of Canadian society.

The costs of this creative solution illustrate the magnitude of the solution but are quite modest in terms of the benefits and of Canada's overall economic spending. As the Caledon Institute suggests, the net increased costs to the federal government are $1.5 billion for a refundable tax credit and $3.5 billion for the basic income program. The provincial revenue from a refundable tax credit is $0.1 billion and the savings from a basic income program as a result of people leaving social assistance is $2.5 billion. That leaves a total new cost for the basic income program of $2.4 billion, considering these two initiatives together.

The benefits of this proposal are significant. Hundreds of thousands of people will be able to get off stigmatizing social assistance programs and onto an income support program that recognizes the unique poverty-related consequences of disability in Canada. Many more people with disabilities would benefit from a refundable disability tax credit. With a nationwide network of disability supports programs, people with disabilities could get the supports they require in order to get and retain a job, contribute to their communities and raise their families.

The Caledon Institute argues that this is a practical and doable proposal, only lacking in political will. In an era of significant budget cuts and downsizing of public services, governments may not believe that creating a new income program with additional costs would be saleable to the Canadian public. And it is the Canadian public that needs to recognize that our existing approaches, with limited disability supports and use of social assistance as an income support program for people with disabilities, is unsustainable, not only for people with disabilities, but for Canada as a whole. In its 2009 report, the International Labour Office estimated that the economic losses to the Canadian economy resulting from the labour market participation gap were between US$26.6 billion and US$30.6 billion in 2001. Addressing some of these losses through the Caledon Institute proposal, with its $2.4 billion price tag seems a modest investment to transform one aspect of Canadian society.

Belonging and Being Home

Each of the three previous sections focus on measures that governments and society at large can implement to ensure that people with disabilities achieve disability rights in Canada. These measures are critical and have been at the forefront in the work of disability advocates in Canada. But there is something more elusive that is required, something that will not be fixed by a new policy or creative accessibility solutions.

People with disabilities, who have been excluded from Canadian society by institutional barriers and social attitudes and stigma, want to belong. They want to be included. Inclusion, however, is more than adding people with disabilities into society as it exists now. It is about changing and transforming how Canadians think and how Canadian society works so that the diversity of humanity that people with disabilities manifest, isn't highlighted or depicted as unusual or atypical. It is about recognizing and respecting in all relationships — social and individual — the uniqueness of each human being. It is about communities in which people with disabilities live alongside those without disabilities, and each cares about each other's well-being. It is about towns and cities where resources are available so that those who need them can remain with those who love them most and not have to move to receive services. It is about honouring the abilities and contributions of each in mosques, talking circles, community centres, band offices, workplaces, sports teams and churches. It is about celebrating art and culture that engages and reflects disability.

People with disabilities, like most Canadians, want to lead ordinary lives. Calvin Wood, in the introduction to this book, talked about the things that he loves to do — going to Tim's for a coffee, spending time with his friends and working at his job. When people with disabilities belong and are included, they are accepted for who they are as they are. They are not identified as the person with MS, or the poor man who is wheelchair bound, the blind woman, the woman with the capacity of a four-year-old or any other label. In a society where people with disabilities belong, impairments and differences exist but are not the defining feature of an individual.

How do we create communities that embrace and include people with disabilities? How do people with disabilities belong and feel at home in the world in which they live? For people to belong, they need to be home. While home often refers to a physical structure like a house or apartment, being home means a space, with those people closest to us, where we are accepted and affirmed as who we want to be. Home is about our roots, our culture and our identities.

Belonging and being home means having the ability to make one's own decisions and have them respected. The UNCRPD declares that people with disabilities have the right to support when exercising their legal capacity (article 12). This article was developed in part from the example of people in British Columbia who created legal support mechanisms called representation agreements. These agreements enable people who may otherwise have been deemed incompetent to have an alternative to adult guardianship. The agreements give supports for decision-making while at the same time enhancing capabilities and without removing rights. These agreements apply to and enable all adults, not just people with disabilities, in B.C. to plan for the future. With these agreements, people with disabilities in B.C. have been able to show their capacity to make their own decisions with the right supports.

Belonging and being home means being surrounded by people who care about and are interested in you, not only because they get paid to take care of you. In Isaac's story, his mother tells of his desire to live outside of a home defined by disability. Isaac, an adult with autism, lived for years moving from his home to the place where he received disability services, often commuting long distances each week. He was placed in group homes but was not happy. Finally he was able to communicate his wishes to his parents.

> Through Isaac's facilitated communicating, we now understand that he has a very good sense of how he wants to live. For the past few years, he has been centrally involved in making plans for his life. His clear desire to live close to us, in the familiar town that has been our home for almost his whole life, narrows the options a bit. He wants a place that will be his long-term home, shared with several people who believe in him and whom he chooses. His home needs

to be spacious and to have a garden, and it should be in town, on a bus route, and close to open green space for long hikes with his dog Missy...

Isaac's wish to live in his own home, not a group home and not shared with others who are defined by their disabilities, is a big challenge. There are all sorts of worries. Living the way he wants is a new idea for the authorities and for friends who point out all the difficulties. How can he afford all the personal support he needs? What about his special diet and sensory integration? His needs for regular structure and consistency, and for skilled and sensitive support with communication and learning? How can we vet the people who share his house to be sure of their motives and reliability? And what about the neighbours? We start to think that it's all too difficult. But then we remember that all these will be concerns wherever Isaac lives.[5]

Isaac isn't alone in trying to create new ways to belong and be home. Catherine Schaefer pioneered a new model of community living when in 1986 she moved into a house separate from her parents, living in a cooperative arrangement with those who provide support for her living as well as others who did not provide support. When walking around the community of Wolseley in downtown Winnipeg, it is not unusual to see Catherine in her wheelchair with a friend or two, looking in the shops or at the flowers. Catherine is an integral part of her community even though for many years people wondered if she even knew she was there.[6]

L'Arche also illustrates a model of living in an integrated setting with people with disabilities and those who assist them equally responsible for their lives and communities. L'Arche has a vision that is both community-based and transformative, based on the importance of relationships. Jean Vanier, its founder, comments: "Real peace implies something deeper than polite acceptance of those who are different. It means meeting those who are different, appreciating them and their culture, and creating bonds of friendship with them."[7]

These examples illustrate the importance of listening to and respecting the decisions of the individuals with disabilities, who receive strong support from their families and friends and have access to resources to make this a reality. Some resources that help many people with disabilities live as part of communities are the cooperative and community economic development movements. This work focuses on the ability to achieve rights through communities and group initiatives. Carolyn and John Lemon, parents of an adult daughter with intellectual disabilities and activists in the field of cooperatives, outline several cooperative initiatives, in housing and business ventures, among people with intellectual disabilities in Toronto. They suggest that some of the benefits have come because they are a mix of segregated and integrated settings. They recognize

> the need of people with disabilities for contact with others who experience the same challenges they face, as well as for opportunities to participate in the mainstream of daily life. In fact, the mix allows the partners or residents to live in a way more closely aligned to that of most people in all walks of life who spend some of their time with others of a background, language and culture similar to their own, and other time in activities that bring them in touch with people from a variety of backgrounds.[8]

Belonging and being home require communities that include and adapt to the variations of members in those communities. It requires looking beyond the standard and often easier answer to questions of what to do with people with disabilities. It requires looking for solutions that enhance the capacities of individuals to make their own decisions and to live surrounded by people who are interested in and care about them. In reality, it is about finding solutions for inclusion and belonging that make people with disabilities the subject of their own lives and their own rights and that enable them to be active participants in society.

5. LEARNING FROM ORDINARY LIVES, CHANGING SOCIAL ATTITUDES

One of the premises of disability rights is that people with disabilities should enjoy the same human rights as every other person in the world. Yet, because we live in a world created and dominated by people without disabilities, people with disabilities face barriers, discrimination and stigma. These have the effect of treating people with disabilities as different, "other" or "abnormal," in contrast with mainstream (that is, non-disabled) society. The goal of disability rights is to identify the barriers as well as measures to promote and enhance the human rights of people with disabilities in the context of these barriers.

Yet even in framing disability rights as about bridging gaps between people with and without disabilities, we highlight what is different based in disability. Often this reinforces the belief that having disability means that you are different, which in turn means that you are less than someone without that difference and that as a person with disabilities you have less to offer the world.

When we equate the differences of disabilities with negative or undesirable experiences, we reduce people with disabilities to lesser citizens. But when we recognize the diversity of humanity that disability and impairment illustrate, we reject the fantasy that able-bodied people are "whole," "invulnerable" or "normal." Instead, we recognize a diverse and complex humanity with many forms of bodies, including bodies with impairments. This rich version of humanity allows us to see people with disabilities as full of possibilities and potential. This does not make disabled people into "supercrips" or heroic people who combat obstacles and triumph as an inspiration to the rest of us. Nor is it an assumption that people with disabilities are endowed with extraordinary gifts of wisdom or insight as a result of their disabilities.

This understanding of a rich, complex and diverse humanity enables us to look at ordinary life and people who live ordinary lives, including experiences with disabilities. Ordinary life includes getting up in the morning, having breakfast, getting dressed, going to work or school or however we occupy our time. It includes playing with children and doing the chores associated with home, child or elder care. It includes having fun, however we define it — bowling, reading, being on the Internet. This is the stuff of ordinary life. In this, experiences of disability become a teacher of the diverse experiences of humanity, as Tanya Titchkosky, a disability studies scholar, reminds us.[1]

Experiences of disability in ordinary life teach us all more about being human by asserting the variations of humanity — exemplifying adaptation and ingenuity when faced with challenges, change and complexity and illustrating interconnectedness.[2]

Being Human

Media images, our communities and neighbourhoods, government programs and what we learn in our families and schools all shape our understanding of what it means to be human. Being human is often portrayed as being independent, active, healthy, smart and contributing. The lives of people with disabilities challenge the meanings commonly associated with these characteristics and values. They force us to recognize greater variation among humans and value these differences.

Many people with disabilities use devices or aids to lead their ordinary lives. These may include wheelchairs, ventilators, prosthetic limbs or feeding tubes. For many people without disabilities, these aids may appear to prevent independence or seem to be too great an intrusion into what is "naturally" human. This may be in part because we try to put ourselves there, having to rely on those devices. With that imagining, we meet our own discomfort with and perhaps fear of the loss of independence. We do not want to be in a place where we rely on a ventilator or are incontinent and have to wear diapers or have someone wipe our bums. For many, that would not be a quality of life they believe they could or would like to live.

Robert Latimer thought that putting a feeding tube to assist Tracy Latimer with nutrition was too much intervention, a mutilation, of Tracy's body. For many people with disabilities, feeding tubes are not a source of artificial nutrition — but provide breakfast, lunch and supper. The feeding tube may liberate someone who has difficulty swallowing or getting enough nourishment through their mouths. Jim Derksen told the story of his friend David's use of a feeding tube:

> My friend David had always been able to eat through his mouth, but as his disability progressed, he began eating pureed food to avoid aspiration. He became very malnourished at one point several years ago and decided to go to a feeding tube. I spoke to him at the time that Terry Schiavo was in the media. I asked David, when he got up in the morning and was having some food, what did he call that? He said, "I call it breakfast, and when I eat later in the day, I call it lunch and dinner." It's just simply that these are different ways of being liberated.[3]

By portraying feeding tubes and the use of other devices as artificial or "unnatural," some have argued that those who have to use these devices are suffering and we should end that suffering. That is what Robert Latimer argued in justifying his murder of Tracy. But, as with David, Sam Filer told of how these technologies liberated him and his family to a quality of life and level of ability he had not previously imagined.

In living life with ventilators, feeding tubes, diapers and wheel-chairs, people with disabilities are expanding our images of humanity to include life with these adaptations. This enables people without disabilities to look at the potential use of a wheelchair or other device in their own lives, with the realization that their quality of living with impairment can be enhanced with the right supports.

People who require supported decision-making teach similar lessons about how we understand human competence and intelligence. In Canada, many believe that only a person who is competent and rational or intelligent can make independent decisions. We value independence greatly and fight to keep our own independence throughout life. We measure intelligence and label those who measure low on those scales as intellectually disabled. We have placed people with those labels in institutions and have certified them as "incapable" or "incompetent." With these labels in place, others make decisions on their behalf. Not only are they disabled and incompetent, but they are also dependent. Often people with these labels are silent as well because they do not communicate verbally. Even if they could say what they wanted, it is likely they would not be heard or accepted because of the multiple labels that have been attached to them.

Justin Clark rejected his family's attempt to have him labelled mentally incompetent after living sixteen years in an institution. He took his desire to make his own decisions about his life to court, where in 1982, the court, against the advice of expert witnesses, declared him competent. As Michael Bach, disability studies scholar and executive vice-president of the CACL, argues, it was the personal knowledge of those who provided support to Justin Clark and what Justin communicated through his Blissymbolics Board that were convincing evidence of Justin's capacity.

Rebecca Beayni reminded us, in Chapter 3, of her intelligence and capacity in her presentation to the United Nations Ad Hoc Committee on the Rights and Dignity of Persons with Disabilities. Her presentation further illustrates how she is a teacher of those around her.

> Rebecca continues to disseminate citizenship education in her pursuits as an adult. She has an extremely vigorous calendar of commitments. On Mondays she listens to Grade 1 students read at her old elementary school. This exercise helps the little ones gain confidence in their reading ability. Rebecca cannot speak, and for the children this means they are able to read freely with no expectation of criticism — simply the reassurance of a smiling face. Rebecca is also a facilitator at the Royal Ontario Museum in the Bio-Diversity Hands-On exhibit, helping people discover things that they might otherwise not notice.[4]

We extend our understanding of intelligence and competence when we recognize Rebecca's teaching abilities and Justin's advocacy for independent, supported decision-making. We may experience fear when we think to a time when we may need more support to make decisions about our lives and ask how will we ensure that the decisions we would like are made and respected? These pioneers and teachers illustrate ways forward, including through representation agreements modelled and implemented in British Columbia and circles of cooperative, supported living modelled by Catherine Schaefer.

In asserting the diversity of humanity, people with disabilities expand our understanding of humanity, including variations that require the support of aids and devices or of a community. In declaring their independence and competence, people with disabilities give models to all Canadians about ensuring our voices are heard, our needs are met and our contributions are valued and respected.

Pioneers and Innovators

Experiences with impairments are often, of necessity, teachers of pioneering and innovative ways to deal with barriers and challenges. Each time a child goes into a daycare or school setting that has not had to address similar needs, they become teachers about how to provide support for learning, create inclusive classrooms and playgrounds, and foster respectful and supportive friendships and relationships. Each worker that enters a new workplace or experiences changes in how they interact with their environments, innovates and teaches about accommodations, inclusion and appropriate supports. Through each of life's transitions, inclusion and adaptations need to be renegotiated.

Canadian society does not often equate disability and innovation, yet people with disabilities have pioneered many innovations. Experiences with disabilities are a source of social innovations. Al Etmanski, a disability thinker and activist, suggests we understand social innovation as collective and creative responses to pressing and persistent social issues and concerns.[5] Thinking about social innovation leads us to ask questions like: What is the society we imagine? Should we be doing something different, not more of the same? Our responses come in large part from our experiences in life — not from abstracted thinking about problems and solutions. Al suggests: "We are compelled to innovate because we want the best for those we love, because we want to decrease suffering and hardship, because we want to nurture a good life and a good death. We are inspired to a higher standard of creativity and ingenuity by the daily challenges we face in taking care of each other."

These relationships of caring and support lead to people to innovate for a number of reasons. Al has compiled the following list:

- the impossible is unacceptable
- they innovate from the heart, with the heart
- they are on the front lines living with challenges, years

and sometimes decades before they seep into the consciousness of systems and institutions

- their creativity accumulates over time — the perfect conditions for repeated experimentation leading to breakthroughs
- their incentive for groundbreaking, disruptive innovations comes from what they experience and what they witness. Incremental changes often won't do for friends and loved ones
- their resources are limited so they know how to stretch a dollar, and still be innovative
- their care is voluntary and freely given — their commitment is beyond the boundaries of job descriptions, office hours, strategic plans, funding, fashion, business and political priorities
- they are both consumers and producers — they know the system inside out; what works and what doesn't and how to realize the untapped potential of what you may already be offering.[6]

Al Etmanski speaks clearly from his work in the family-based disability movement. He has been at the forefront of creating the Registered Disability Savings Plans (RDSP) in Canada, an innovation to address the concerns of parents of children with intellectual disabilities who worried about who would care for their adult children when they died. But it is not only in relationships of care and support that innovation happens.

Innovation happens when people with disabilities, individually and collectively, push for recognition or claim their right to be present. The advocacy voices of people with disabilities, through their representative organizations, like the CCD, People First, the National Network for Mental Health and the DisAbled Women's Network (DAWN), are ongoing pioneering and innovative collective presences transforming Canadian society. Air and rail travel will not be the same because of the persistence of the CCD all the way to the Supreme Court of Canada. DAWN Canada has challenged the laws governing evidence that require women labelled intellectually or mentally disabled to prove that they understand what it means to tell the truth, including in cases of sexual abuse.[7] The advocacy work of disability organizations made certain that disability rights were part of the Canadian Charter of Rights and Freedoms, even when politicians told them the words did not need to be there, the rights would still be protected.

Innovation was required to imagine and create policy mechanisms that could be used to support independent living and ensure control of the services received by people with disabilities themselves. Direct payments and self-managed care are now standard features of service delivery across Canada, thanks to the imagination and persistence of many people with disabilities in the independent living movement. Representation agreements were innovative responses to the need for mechanisms to provide supported decision-making.

Innovation happens when people with disabilities meet barriers to their involvement or have to adapt to systems and policies that do not include them. In addressing the complexity that is required to include and address their needs, novel solutions are identified. In many ways, the adaptability to change and complexity that many people with disabilities model in meeting a world full of barriers is an example for all people in how to address change. In a study of disability and cancer care, providers noted that when people with existing impairments get cancer, they tend to be more skilled at coping with the health care system, are better informed about their treatment and treatment needs, and adjust better to the effects of cancer. In addition, some of the people with disabilities in the study noted that the supports they had developed related to their experiences with disabilities enabled them to provide teaching and support to other people experiencing cancer care.[8]

Experiences with disability have much to teach about how to flourish in a world of complexity and change. They teach about how to work to transform systems and ways of doing things so that all can benefit. They teach about the importance of collective action and of ensuring "nothing about us without us."

We Are Connected

Experiences with disability are an extraordinary teacher of how to deal with bodies that don't always work the way we wish they would and of finding novel or innovative approaches to long-standing issues and concerns. Experiences with disabilities also teach us much about how we are connected to each other and how those interconnections shape all our lives.

Much of the rhetoric of neoliberal (that is, economic conservative) governments and policies and, indeed, Canadian society begins from the premise that we are individual, independent, self-sufficient people. The role of government is to protect that independence and capability. In this type of society, people are created as either capable or not-capable. We recognize capable people as strong, able-bodied, contributing individuals. Disabled people are often portrayed as not-capable.

> The not-capable do not possess their own capacities, whether because they are not "in control of their minds or bodies," or because they must rely on others to facilitate their attainment of their capacities. People with disabilities obviously fall in the not-capable category. People who require attendant care to manage their bodily functions are not capable because they would die if they did not have attendants. People with psychiatric illnesses are not capable because they may not be able to manage their own affairs. People who are deaf are not capable because they may not communicate in an oral language without interpretation. The underlying belief in the independence of every individual separates people with disabilities from the rest

of society and excludes them from the benefits of society and of state protection.[9]

The independent living movement rejected this equation of disability and lack of independence. Rather it has shown how independence is about being able to achieve goals and have control over one's own life. As one disability studies scholar wrote, "independence is not linked to the physical or intellectual capacity to care for oneself without assistance; independence is created by having assistance when and how one requires it."[10]

In earlier parts of this book, we were given stories about how Rebecca Beayni and Catherine Schaefer live their lives and are able to achieve their goals with supports provided in relationships. Rebecca's presentation to the United Nations asks:

> How does a person who is non-verbal and wheel-chair-bound, living within the constraints of others' ideas and expectations of people with disabilities, do all these things? Her success in overcoming obstacles is mainly due to the deep and committed relationships she has developed with family, friends, her support circle, as well as collaboration with community groups that she comes in contact with regularly such as the church, schools and other venues. Her support circle, who have been meeting regularly for the past 13 years, help interpret her goals and dreams.
>
> Rebecca does not speak, so those around her ensure that she has many other ways to express her feelings and desires. It is imperative that she have long term relationships, both paid and unpaid, who can help build the capacity of the community to welcome her gifts. In return, Rebecca helps them create a better world for all. This is citizenship, and Rebecca is an esteemed educator in this regard.[11]

In each of these cases, the work of providing support also means interpreting their goals to others, since each of these people are not able to say what their goals are. Yet they remain people with human rights. The neoliberal and individualistic understanding of independent personhood is unable to address the complexity of Rebecca's and Catherine's lives and leaves us questioning whether they can really be considered persons. But when we expand our understanding of humanity, when we recognize the interdependence required to live a human life, including a life with disabilities, we begin to understand that independence as self-sufficiency is a fiction. Independence is a fiction for people with disabilities who require assistance to lead ordinary lives, as well as for people without disabilities, since we all need the assistance of and relationships with other people to live our lives.

In the realization that we live in a world of relationships, where we provide and receive assistance and support to each other, we also learn about how we are connected or interdependent. In that recognition of the relational nature of our ordinary lives, we break down the barriers between "us," people without disabilities, and "them," people with disabilities.

The recognition may begin as simply as "they" are part of "our" lives. In the 2004 Environics public opinion survey of Canadians about disability issues, 75 percent of those surveyed said that they have a family member or friend with disabilities. That is significant. Most Canadians already have people with disabilities in their lives. The survey also illustrated that these are often not close relationships, often outside of immediate family and not someone with whom they live. As Michael Prince suggests in commenting on the results of this survey, it is more likely "a silent relation between us" or solidarity among strangers.

This solidarity may lead to recognizing encounters with disability in public spaces. Over the time this book was gestating, I kept a journal, writing the stories of disability in everyday life I encountered or recognized. This story illustrates that silent relation or connection between us.

September 30, 2009

I was at the National Gallery in Ottawa and had to use the washroom. An older man was in the women's washroom, holding a stall door closed. A number of women came in. He said it was a long story, a bit embarrassed and trying to explain his presence there. I asked if I could take over the job for him. He agreed and said he would wait outside. The very old woman he was helping came out of the stall and needed some help figuring out how to use the automatic faucet and soap dispenser. I showed her how to use it and she washed her hands. I got her some paper towels. "Not too many!" she said. After she dried her hands, she wiped the granite countertops. She kept drying and wiping them until I gently reminded her that she had someone waiting for her outside. I walked with her to the door and the man met us and thanked me. Later as I was leaving the gallery, I saw the two again. She was in a wheelchair with a group of people who used wheelchairs. He smiled at me — again thanking me for the ordinary, everyday support and kindness.

Experiences with disability also teach us that each and every one of us has a body that requires adaptation and accommodation. At any moment, we may experience environments that do not adapt to our individual needs, including as our body changes as a result of accidents, genetic coding or our unique ways of being. In other words, "we" are "them." That recognition of the troublesomeness of bodies is often the fear that drives eugenic practices and euthanasia. "We" don't want to become "them" and live in a world that devalues and restricts our independence. To live with the possibility of disability and impairment is frightening and often prevents "us" from accepting "them." Keeping "them" separate and not recognizing our interconnections, helps "us" maintain the fiction that "we" do not need anyone, that "we" are independent. On the other hand, recognizing that "we" are "them" can lead to empathy, recognizing the nature of the barriers and challenges associated with living with disabilities in an able-bodied world and acting in solidarity or support.

Another encounter I had illustrates a grandfather's acts of solidarity with his son and grandson in their experiences with barriers and disabilities.

July 2009, Spruce Sands Beach, Manitoba

I was sitting with my kids on the sandy beach by our cottage. Only a few people were at the beach. One was an older gentleman who seemed to be watching his grandson in the water. While I watched my son swimming, the man commented out of the blue "My grandson has autism and I'm looking after him to give my son a break." I didn't know what to say and commented that I was sure his son appreciated his support. He agreed. We stayed in our own worlds until two events happened. He asked his grandson to come in and have a snack. He spoke each word precisely, pointed to the juice box and used a sign for drinking. The boy kept playing in the water. The grandfather continued in his efforts with increasing insistency. Finally the boy smashed the water, made a loud noise and looked at his grandfather. Then the grandfather gave the boy some juice.

We talked after that, the grandfather and I, about the boy's speech, his use of symbols. The grandfather told me about the one-on-one training to get his grandson to acquire some language, about the sheer physicality of caring for the boy and how his son was bone weary. He said his grandson loved the water and therefore they spent as much time as possible at the cottage.

A little later the boy was in the water and the grandfather seemed upset. He ran around the boy trying to get

> him out of the water and covered. It seems the boy had taken off his bathing suit and was naked in the water. The grandfather called others from the family to help, to bring clothes. They were agitated, all trying to help. In the end, once the others were all gone, the boy let his grandfather put his suit back on and they went home.

In my ordinary life, I encountered a grandfather who needed to speak of his love for his grandson and son, his worry about the demands on his son, his relief at being able to be of some use in a family that was strained by the demands and the barriers they face in response to his grandson's autism and his happiness that his grandson had a place like the beach where he could play in the water. I was honoured to witness this solidarity and empathy, and my life was made richer through this connection. The grandfather did not act from fear of disability but from a place of love, support and respect.

Recognizing our common and diverse humanity and need for relationship enables us to say "we" are "them" and "they" are "us." In our need for relationship and support, we are human and therefore are interdependent. When we recognize the diversity of our bodies, we remove the barriers between "us" and "them."

Marion Kerans writes of her own transformation as a mother of a son who acquired multiple sclerosis and died at age forty-five. She speaks of her denial of his condition and attempts to do things for him as a way of compensating, coming to an acceptance that this was a part of life and respecting and supporting his independence and direction for how he wanted to live life:

> When Patrick got the diagnosis in late October of 1984 he was crushed. Pat and I persuaded him to come home to Halifax for a month's holiday. We witnessed his sudden unsteady gait and even inability to walk when his energy abandoned him. With his enthusiasm gone, there was only

confusion in its wake. He did not know what he was going to do with himself. I tried to focus on how we could help him. It seemed I always concentrated on that, rather than on his disease. I suppose it was my form of denial. I would learn slowly in the years ahead to acknowledge his condition and to take my leads from him about how he might be helped.[12]

In the end, Marion's son Patrick spoke of how he wanted to lead by example in preparing for death, recognizing the humanity that linked them and the reality that death is a universal human experience:

It is so weird even now to talk about my dying, but it is not something I am frightened of. I can only hope that the example I have set for my family members gives them courage when they go forward to face their own.[13]

The interconnections illustrated in these stories help us to learn what disability teaches, that we are connected, that it is not about "us" and "them," but that "we" are "them" and "they" are "us" because of our shared and diverse humanity through ordinary life and until death.

SOURCES FOR FURTHER READING

Chouinard, Vera. 2010. "Women with Disabilities' Experiences of Government Employment Assistance in Canada." *Disability and Rehabilitation* 32 (2): 148–58.

Chouinard, Vera, and Valerie Crooks. 2005. "'Because *They* Have All the Power and I Have None': State Restructuring of Income and Employment Supports and Disabled Women's Lives in Ontario, Canada." *Disability and Society* 20, 1 (Jan.): 19–32.

Community Living Manitoba. 2007. *When Bad Things Happen: Violence, Abuse, Neglect and other Mistreatments against Manitoban Women with Intellectual Disabilities*. Winnipeg: Community Living Manitoba.

Crompton, Susan. 2011 "Women with Activity Limitation" in *Women in Canada: A Gender-based Statistical Report*. Ottawa: Ministry of Industry.

Crooks, Valerie, Vera Chouinard, and Robert D. Wilton. 2008. "Understanding, Embracing, Rejecting: Women's Negotiations of Disability Constructions and Categorizations after Becoming Chronically Ill." *Social Science & Medicine* 67 11: 1837–46.

Davis, Lennard (ed.). 2010. *The Disability Studies Reader*. Third edition. New York: Routledge.

Dossa, Parin. 2009. *Racialized Bodies, Disabling Worlds: Storied Lives of Immigrant Muslim Women*. Toronto: University of Toronto Press.

Driedger, Diane (ed.). 2010. *Living the Edges: A Disabled Women's Reader*. Toronto: Ianna Publications.

Durst, Douglas, Shelly Manuel South, and Mary Bluechardt. 2006. "Urban First Nations People with Disabilities Speak Out." *Journal of Aboriginal Health* September: 34–43.

Jongbloed, Lyn. 2003. "Disability Policy in Canada: An Overview." *Journal of Disability Policy Studies* 13: 203.

Lord, John, and Peggy Hutchinson. 2003. "Individualised Supports and Funding." *Disability & Society* 18, 1: 71–86.

Malacrida, Claudia. 2009. "Performing Motherhood in a Disablist World: Dilemmas of Motherhood, Femininity and Disability." *International Journal of Qualitative Studies in Education* 22, 1: 99–117.

Morrow, M., et al. 2009. "Removing Barriers to Work: Building Economic Security for People with Psychiatric Disabilities." *Critical Social Policy* 29, 4: 655–76.

Neufeldt, A.H., and H. Enns (eds.). 2003. *In Pursuit of Equal Participation: Canada and Disability at Home and Abroad*. Toronto: Captus Press.

Pothier, Dianne, and R. Devlin (eds.). 2006. *Critical Disability Theory: Essays in Philosophy, Politics, Policy and Law*. Vancouver: UBC Press.

Prince, Michael J. 2009. *Absent Citizens: Disability Politics and Policy in Canada*. Toronto: University of Toronto Press.

Stienstra, Deborah, and Aileen Wight-Felske (eds.). 2003. *Making Equality: History of Advocacy and Persons with Disabilities in Canada*. Toronto: Captus Press.

Strong-Boag, Veronica. 2007. "'Children of Adversity': Disabilities and Child Welfare in Canada from the Nineteenth to the Twenty-First Century." *Journal of Family History* 32: 413

Titchkosky, Tanya. 2003. *Disability, Self and Society*. Toronto: University of Toronto Press.

Titchkosky, Tanya, and Rod Michalko (eds.). 2009. *Rethinking Normalcy: A Disability Studies Reader.* Toronto: Canadian Scholars Press.

Vick, A., and E. Lightman. 2010. "Barriers to Employment among Women with Complex Episodic Disabilities." *Journal of Disability Policy Studies* 21, 2: 70–80.

NOTES

Introduction

1.   Calvin Wood, 2010, "Poverty and Disability: My Lived Experience," presented to Disabling Poverty/Enabling Citizenship: End Exclusion 2010 conference, Caledon Institute of Social Policy, <http://www.caledoninst.org/Publications/PDF/909ENG.pdf>.

2.   Statistics Canada, 2007, *Participation and Activity Limitation Survey 2006: Analytical Report*, Ottawa: Minister of Industry.

3.   Quoted in Yvonne Peters, 2007, *The Canadian Human Rights Commission Strives to Design a New Business Model: What Does This Mean for Persons with Disabilities?* Winnipeg: Council of Canadians with Disabilities, <http://www.ccdonline.ca/en/humanrights/promoting/new-business-model>.

4.   Canadian Human Rights Commission, 2006, *Annual Report 2005*, Ottawa: Minister of Public Works and Government Services, p. 20.

5.   Marie White, 2009, "An Open Letter to Members of Parliament: The Value of the Canadian Human Rights Commission to People with Disabilities" <http://www.ccdonline.ca/en/humanrights/promoting/open-letter-value-of-hr-system-5October2009>.

6.   *Globe and Mail*, November 21, 2008, "Actual, Bearable Accommodations," <http://www.theglobeandmail.com/news/opinions/actual-bearable-accommodations/article723934/>.

Chapter 1

1. Marcia H. Rioux, 2009, "Bending Towards Justice," in T. Titchkosky and R. Michalko (eds.), *Rethinking Normalcy: A Disability Studies Reader*, Toronto: Canadian Scholars Press.

2. Aldred H. Neufeldt, 2003, "Disability in Canada: An Historical Perspective," in Henry Enns and Aldred H. Neufeldt (eds.), *In Pursuit of Equal Participation: Canada and Disability at Home And Abroad*, Toronto: Captus Press.

3. Henry Enns and Yutta Fricke, 2003, "The Emergence of a Global Disability Rights Movement," in Henry Enns and Aldred H. Neufeldt (eds.), *In Pursuit of Equal Participation: Canada and Disability at Home and Abroad*, Toronto: Captus Press; and Diane Driedger, 1989, *The Last Civil Rights Movement: Disabled Peoples' International*, New York: St. Martin's Press.

4. April D'Aubin, 2003, "'Nothing About Us Without Us': CCD's Struggle for the Recognition of a Human Rights Approach to Disability Issues," in Henry Enns and Aldred H. Neufeldt, p. 120.

5. For a description of the historical development of independent living in Canada, see John Lord, 2010, *Impact: Changing the Way We View Disability*, Ottawa: Independent Living Canada; and Cassandra Phillips, 2003, "Steering Your Own Ship: The Growth of Individual Advocacy Within the Canadian Association of Independent Living Centres," in D. Stienstra and A. Wight-Felske (eds.), *Making Equality: History of Advocacy and Persons with Disabilities in Canada*, Toronto: Captus Press, pp. 197–219.

6. Melanie Panitch, 2008, *Disability, Mothers and Organization: Accidental Activists*, New York: Routledge.

7. Michael J. Prince, 2009, *Absent Citizens: Disability Politics and Policy in Canada*, Toronto: University of Toronto Press, pp. 112–33.

8. Council of Canadians with Disabilities (CCD), n.d., "From Vision to Action: Building an Inclusive and Accessible Canada: A National Action Plan," <http://www.ccdonline.ca/en/socialpolicy/actionplan/inclusive-accessible-canada>.

9. Deborah Stienstra, 2003, "'Listen, Really Listen, to Us': Consultation, Disabled People and Governments in Canada," in D. Stienstra and A. Wight-Felske (eds.), *Making Equality*.

10. Laurie Beachell, 1992, "Mainstream '92," *Abilities Magazine* Winter, <http://www.abilities.ca/social_policy/1992/12/01/mainstream_92/>.

11. For further information, see Social Union, n.d., "Background Information on the Employability Assistance for People with Disabilities Initiative," <http://www.unionsociale.gc.ca/pwd/eapd-bg_e.html>.

12. Federal/Provincial/Territorial Ministers Responsible for Social Services (FPT), 1998, "In Unison: A Canadian Approach to Disability Issues — A Vision Paper," <http://www.unionsociale.gc.ca/pwd/unison/unison_e.html>.

13. Michael J. Prince, 2004, "Canadian Disability Policy: Still a Hit-and-Miss Affair," *Canadian Journal of Sociology/Cahiers canadiens de sociologie* 29(1): 66.

14. Human Resources and Skills Development Canada (HRSDC), 2011, "Labour Market Agreements for Persons with Disabilities," <http://www.hrsdc.gc.ca/eng/disability_issues/labour_market_agreements/index.shtml>.

15. Technical Advisory Committee on Tax Measures for Persons with Disabilities, <http://www.disabilitytax.ca/main-e.html>.

16. Council of Canadians with Disabilities (CCD), 2011, "Federal Poverty Reduction Plan Must Address Disability Poverty," *A Voice of Our Own* 29, 1, <http://www.ccdonline.ca/en/publications/voice/2011/03>; and Michael Mendelson, Ken Battle, Sherri Torjman and Ernie Lightman, 2010, *A Basic Income Plan for Canadians with Severe Disabilities*, Toronto: Caledon Institute for Social Policy, <http://www.caledoninst.org/Publications/Detail/?ID=906>.

17. Prince Edward Island, Department of Community Services, Seniors and Labour, 2011, "Supports for People with Disabilities," <http://www.gov.pe.ca/sss/index.php3?number=1018613>.

18. Don Shackel, 2008, "The Experiences of First Nations People with Disabilities and Their Families in Receiving Services and Supports in First Nations Community in Manitoba: Honouring the Stories," Masters thesis, Disability Studies, University of Manitoba, pp. 37–38.

19. Cameron Crawford, 2010, "Disabling Poverty and Enabling Citizenship: Understanding the Poverty and Exclusion of Canadians with Disabilities," <http://ccdonline.ca/en/socialpolicy/poverty-citizenship/demographic-profile/understanding-poverty-exclusion>.

20. Don Shackel, "The Experiences," 2008, p. 39.

21. First Nations Child and Family Caring Society of Canada (FNCFCS), 2011, "Jordan's Principle: Joint Declaration of Support for Jordan's Principle to Resolving Jurisdictional Disputes Affecting Services to First

Nations Children," <http://www.fncfcs.com/jordans-principle>.

22. Don Shackel, 2011, "First Nations Disability and Inclusive Education Supports: Critical Reflection on Jordan's Principle," unpublished.

23. Don Shackel, "The Experiences," 2008, p. 85.

Chapter 2

1. Christie Blatchford, 2011, "Inquest Last Chance to Get Full Story of Ashley Smith Tragedy," *Globe and Mail*, April 2, p. A2.

2. Howard Sapers, 2008, *A Preventable Death*, Office of the Correctional Investigator, <http://www.oci-bec.gc.ca/rpt/oth-aut/oth-aut20080620-eng.aspx>.

3. Kopstein, Robert L. 2003. "Report on the Inquest and Recommendations Related to the Death of Cory Moar," Winnipeg: Provincial Court of Manitoba.

4. *R. v. Latimer*, 2001, SCC 1, [2001] 1 S.C.R. 3 Robert William Latimer v. Her Majesty the Queen, January 18, <http://scc.lexum.org/en/2001/2001scc1/2001scc1.html>.

5. Andy Johnson, 2011. "Latimer: No Regrets About Killing Disabled Daughter," <http://www.ctv.ca/CTVNews/TopStories/20110307/latimer-ctv-interview-1100307/>.

6. People First of Canada and Canadian Association for Community Living, 2010, *Institution Watch*, 5, 3 (Fall).

7. Michael Tutton, 2009, "Cabinet Minister 'Shocked' at Abuse of Mentally Disabled in N.S," *Daily Gleaner*, Dec. 7, <http://dailygleaner.canadaeast.com/rss/article/881126>.

8. Lisa Priest, 2004, "Nursing Homes No Answer for the Young," *Globe and Mail*, Dec 18, p. A13.

9. Lisa Priest, 2004, "It's Not Where I Should Be. It Feels Degrading," *Globe and Mail*, Dec. 18, p. A14.

10. Madeleine Vallée, 2008, "Escapes from the Nursing Home," *Globe and Mail*, Nov. 5. p. L6.

11. Helen Henderson, 2008, "Man's 1981 Fight Made Headlines," *The Star*, March 15, <http://www.thestar.com/article/339391>.

12. Council of Canadians with Disabilities (CCD), 2003, *Annual Report: 2002–2003*, <http://www.ccdonline.ca/en/about/board/annualreports/2003>.

13. United Nations Enable, n.d., "Chapter Six: From Provisions to Practice: Implementing the Convention, Legal Capacity and Supported Decision-

Making," <http://www.un.org/disabilities/default.asp?id=242>.

14. Heidi L. Janz, 1998, "Disabling Images and the Dangers of Public Perception: A Commentary on the Media's 'Coverage' of the *Latimer* Case," *Constitutional Forum*, 9, 3, pp. 66–70.

15. Z.M. Lutfiyya, K.D. Schwartz, and N. Hansen, 2009, "False Images: Re-framing the End-of-Life Portrayal of Disability in the Film *Million Dollar Baby*," in Sandra Shapsay (ed.), *Bioethics at the Movies*, Baltimore: Johns Hopkins University Press, pp. 225–55.

16. Sam Filer, n.d., "Speech of Hope: Quality of Life — Who's the judge?" <http://www.alsforums.com/forum/stories-hope/13713-speech-hope-quality-life-who-s-judge.html>.

Chapter 3

1. Statistics Canada, 2008, *Participation and Activity Limitation Survey 2006: Families of Children with Disabilities in Canada*, Ottawa: Ministry of Industry.

2. Child Care Advocacy Association of Canada, 2004, "What Do We Mean by Inclusion?" Ottawa, <http://www.ccaac.ca/pdf/resources/factsheets/inclusion.pdf>.

3. Human Resources and Skills Development Canada, 2009, *2009 Federal Disability Report: Advancing the Inclusion of People with Disabilities*, Ottawa: Human Resources and Skills Development Canada.

4. Statistics Canada, 2008, *Participation and Activity Limitation Survey 2006: A Profile of Education for Children with Disabilities in Canada*, Ottawa: Ministry of Industry.

5. Statistics Canada, 2008, *Participation: A Profile of Education.*

6. Human Resources and Skills Development Canada, 2009, *2009 Federal Disability Report.*

7. Council of Ministers of Education of Canada (CMEC), n.d., "Education in Canada: Ministerial Priorities in Education," <http://www.cmec.ca/pages/canadawide.aspx#10>.

8. Human Resources and Skills Development Canada, 2009, *2009 Federal Disability Report*, p. 27.

9. T. Chambers, M. Sukai, and M. Bolton, 2011, *Assessment of Debt Load and Financial Barriers Affecting Students with Disabilities in Canadian Postsecondary Education — Ontario Report*, Toronto: Higher Education Quality Council of Ontario.

10. Human Resources and Skills Development Canada, 2009, *2009 Federal*

Disability Report.

11. Stephanie MacLean, Craig McKinnon, and Lois Miller, 2008, *Revisiting Accessibility to Learning: Challenges and Barriers for Adult Learners with Disabilities in Atlantic Canada*, Halifax: Canadian Council on Learning and Independent Living Resource Centre.

12. N.L. Hutchinson, 2010, *Inclusion of Exceptional Learners in Canadian Schools: A Practical Handbook for Teachers*, third edition, Toronto: Pearson Education Canada.

13. Dianne Pothier, 2006, "Eaton v. Brant County Board of Education," *Canadian Journal of Women and the Law*, 18, pp. 121–42.

14. Statistics Canada, 2008, *Participation and Activity Limitation Survey 2006: Labour Force Experience of People with Disabilities in Canada*, Ottawa: Ministry of Industry. The government cancelled the Participation and Activity Limitation Survey in 2010.

15. Organization for Economic Co-operation and Development (OECD), 2010, *Sickness, Disability and Work: Breaking the Barriers*, Canada: Opportunities for Collaboration, Paris: OECD.

16. Disability Rights Promotion International Canada, 2010, "Toronto Monitoring Fact Sheet: Monitoring the Human Rights of People with Disabilities in Canada," <http://www.yorku.ca/drpi/CanadaPublications.html>.

17. Deborah Stienstra, C. Watters, H. Grant, H. Huang, and L. Troschuk, 2004, *Women with Disabilities: Accessing Trade*, Ottawa: Status of Women Canada, <http://publications.gc.ca/pub?id=258150&sl=0>, p. 27.

18. Human Resources and Skills Development Canada (HRSDC), 2010, "2010 Federal Disability Report: The Government of Canada's Annual Report on Disability Issues," Ottawa: Human Resources and Skills Development Canada.

19. Independent Living Resource Centre, 2009, "Why Don't Those People Work?" St. John's, NL: Independent Living Resource Centre, <http://www.ilrc-nl.ca/brochure/sites/default/files/Why Don%27t Those People Work_0.doc>.

20. Cameron Crawford, 2010, "Disabling Poverty."

21. Michael Mendelson et al., 2010, *A Basic Income Plan*.

22. Michael Mendelson et al., 2010, *A Basic Income Plan*.

23. John Stapleton, and Stephanie Procyk, 2010, "A Patchwork Quilt: Income Security for Canadians with Disabilities," *Issue Briefings*, Toronto: Institute for Work and Health.

24. Statistics Canada, 2008, *Participation and Activity Limitation Survey 2006: A Profile of Assistive Technology for People with Disabilities*, Ottawa: Minister of Industry.

25. P. Fournier-Savard, C. Mongeon, and S. Crompton, 2010, "Help with Activities of Daily Living for People with a Disability," *Canadian Social Trends*, October 19, pp. 92–101.

26. Michael Mendelson et al., 2010, *A Basic Income Plan*.

27. Human Resources and Skills Development Canada, 2009, *Employment Equity Act: Annual Report 2008*, Ottawa: Human Resources and Skills Development Canada.

28. Public Service Commission of Canada, 2010, "Employment Equity Designated Group Definitions," <http://jobs-emplois.gc.ca/centres/definitions-eng.htm>.

29. Human Resources and Skills Development Canada, 2009, *Employment Equity Act*.

30. Jean-Louis Deveau, 2008, "Workplace Accommodation for Disabled Workers in the Canadian Federal Public Service: A Textually-Mediated Social Organization," PhD thesis, University of New Brunswick, pp. 212–14.

31. Canadian Human Rights Commission, 2003, *A Place for All: A Guide to Creating an Inclusive Workplace*, Ottawa: Minister of Public Works and Government Services.

32. B. Nelson and Transport Canada, 2010, "Economics of Accessible Transportation in Canada," Paper delivered at the 12th International Conference on Mobility and Transport for Elderly and Disabled Persons (TRANSED 2010), held in Hong Kong on 2–4 June, 2010.

33. Tess Kalinowski, 2007, "Bus Stops Here for TTC," *TheStar.com* July 27, <http://www.thestar.com/News/GTA/article/240400>.

34. David Baker, 2005, *Moving Backwards: Canada's State of Transportation Accessibility in an International Context*, Winnipeg: Council of Canadians with Disabilities.

35. *Council of Canadians with Disabilities v. VIA Rail Canada Inc.*, 2007, 1 S.C.R. 650, 2007 SCC 15, <http://scc.lexum.org/en/2007/2007scc15/2007scc15.html>.

36. Council of Canadians with Disabilities (CCD), 2010, "Student Creates Opportunity to Increase Accessibility," June 2, <http://www.ccdonline.ca/en/transportation/minister/press-release-student-creates-opportunity-2June2010>.

37. Human Resources and Skills Development Canada (HRSDC), 2010, "2010 Federal Disability Report."

38. Canadian Council on Social Development (CCSD), 2002, "Focus on Technology among Persons with Disabilities," *Disability Information Sheet*, 7, <http://www.ccsd.ca/drip/research/dis7/index.htm>.

39. For a description of how this fund came to be see Deborah Stienstra, J. Watzke and G. Birch, 2007, "A Three-Way Dance: The Global Public Good and Accessibility in Information Technologies," *The Information Society*, 23, pp. 149–58.

40. Canadian Radio-Television and Telecommunications Commission (CRTC), 2011, "Letter re: Part VII: Deferral Account Proposal to Improve Accessibility of Mobile Devices and Services," Feb 8, <http://www.crtc.gc.ca/eng/archive/2011/lt110208.htm>.

41. Canadian Radio-Television and Telecommunications Commission (CRTC), 2011, "Change in Effective Control of CTVglobemedia Inc.'s Licensed Broadcasting Subsidiaries," *Broadcasting Decision CRTC 2011-163*, March 7, <http://www.crtc.gc.ca/eng/archive/2011/2011-163.htm>.

42. MaryAnn McColl, Anna Jarzynowska and S.E.D. Shortt, 2010, "Unmet Health Care Needs of People with Disabilities: Population Level Evidence," *Disability and Society* 25, 2, pp. 205–18.

43. Human Resources and Skills Development Canada (HRSDC), 2010, "2010 Federal Disability Report."

44. Human Resources and Skills Development Canada (HRSDC), 2010, "2010 Federal Disability Report."

45. G. Annable, D. Stienstra, and H.M. Chochinov, 2010, "Addressing Disability in Cancer Care," final report to Cancer Journey Action Group, Canadian Partnership Against Cancer, <http://www.partnershipagainstcancer.ca/download/Addressing-disability-in-cancer-care.pdf>.

46. Harvey Max Chochinov, 2007, "Dignity and the Essence of Medicine: The A, B, C, and D of Dignity Conserving Care," *British Medical Journal* 335, pp. 184–87.

47. Joseph Kaufert, R. Wiebe, K. Schwartz, L. Labine, Z.M. Lutfiyya, and C. Pearse, 2010. "End-of-Life Ethics and Disability: Differing Perspectives on Case-Based Teaching," *Medical Health Care and Philosophy* 13, pp 115–26.

48. Tom Shakespeare, L.I. Iezzoni, and N.E. Groce, 2009, "The Art of Medicine: Disability and the Training of Health Professionals," *The Lancet* 374 (November 28), pp. 1815–16.

49. MaryAnn McColl, S. Shortt, D. Hunter, J. Dorland, M. Godwin, W. Rosser, and R. Shaw, 2010, "Access and Quality of Primary Care for People with Disabilities: A Comparison of Practice Factors," *Journal of Disability Policy Studies* 21, 3, pp. 131–40.

Chapter 4

1. Canadian Centre on Disability Studies (CCDS), n.d., "Visitability Canada," <http://www.visitablehousingcanada.com/>.
2. Roeher Institute, 2002, *Moving in Unison into Action: Towards a Policy Strategy for Improving Access to Disability Supports*, Toronto.
3. Environics, 2004, "Canadian Attitudes Towards Disability Issues" (report no. PN 5431), Ottawa, ON: Office for Disability Issues.
4. Social Union, 2005, "News Release: Ministers Meet to Discuss Collaborative Work on Social Issues," <http://www.socialunion.gc.ca/news/201005_e.html>.
5. Ontario Adult Autism Research and Support Network, 2001, "Isaac's Story," <http://www.ont-autism.uoguelph.ca/Isaac's Story.pdf>.
6. Nicola Schaefer, Catherine's mother, wrote about Catherine's life in a book called *Does She Know She's There?* The 1997 update is retitled *Yes! She Knows She's Here*. Inclusion Press.
7. L'Arche Canada, 2011, "Our Vision," <http://www.larche.ca/en/larche/our_vision>.
8. C. Lemon and J. Lemon, 2003, "Community-Based Cooperative Ventures for Adults with Intellectual Disabilities," *The Canadian Geographer,* 47, 4, pp. 414–28.

Chapter 5

1. T. Titchkosky, 2003, *Disability, Self, and Society,* Toronto: University of Toronto Press.
2. These way finders were first identified in Deborah Stienstra and T. Ashcroft, 2010, "Voyaging on the Seas of Spirit: An Ongoing Journey to Understand Disability and Humanity," *Disability and Society* 25, 2, pp. 191–203.
3. Vulnerable Persons and End of Life Care New Emerging Team (VP-NET), 2006, "Report on the First VP-NET Spring Institute: A Good Life Until the End: Palliative Care and People with Disabilities," <http://www.umanitoba.ca/outreach/vpnet/about-events-spring.htm>.

4. Rebecca Beayni, 2005, "Rebecca's Presentation to the United Nations Ad Hoc Committee on the Rights and Dignity of Persons with Disabilities," <http://www.rebeccabeayni.com/AboutMe_PresentationtoUnitedNations.html>.

5. Al Etmanski's blog is at <http://www.aletmanski.com/al-etmanski/>.

6. Al Etmanski, 2011, "'Passionate Amateurs' a Primary Source of Social Innovation," April 25 <http://www.aletmanski.com/al-etmanski/2011/04/the-role-of-passionate-amateurs-in-social-innovation.html>.

7. Daphne Bramham, 2011, "Evidence Rules Leave Disabled Canadian Girls Open to Sex Abuse," *Vancouver Sun* May 30, <http://www.canada.com/vancouversun/news/editorial/story.html?id=5742d57c-1b9e-4092-a925-84eb4fb48434>.

8. Annable et al., 2010, "Addressing Disability."

9. Deborah Stienstra, 2002, "Disabling Globalization: Rethinking Global Political Economy with a Disability Lens," *Global Society*, 16, 2, pp. 109–21.

10. J. Morris, 1993, *Independent Lives? Community Care and Disabled People*, London: Macmillan Press.

11. Rebecca Beayni, 2005, "Rebecca's Presentation."

12. W.J. Patrick Kellerman, n.d., "Writing on the Insides of My Eyelids," <http://www.umanitoba.ca/outreach/vpnet/LD-patrick.htm>.

13. W.J. Patrick Kellerman, n.d., "Writing."

INDEX